Food Flowers Medicine

And Other Gifts From the Garden

Edited by Stacy Russo and Julie Artman

Wild Librarian Press
Santa Ana, California

Copyright © 2025 by Wild Librarian Press

Introduction copyright © 2025 by Stacy Russo

ALL RIGHTS RESERVED

No portion of this work may be reproduced in any form without prior written permission from Wild Librarian Press or its individual author contributors who retain their copyright, except as expressly permitted by U.S. copyright law.

Library of Congress Control Number: 2024922980
Paperback ISBN: 978 – 1-7376759 – 5-2

Statement on Non-Harming Language: The editors made their best, committed effort to review plant names and their meanings and derivations in order to publish a work that is free of words that may be harming or insensitive to readers.

Book design by Sarah E. Holroyd (https://sleepingcatbooks.com)
Cover art *Out in the Moon Garden* by Stacy Russo

Published by Wild Librarian Press, Santa Ana, California

www.wildlibrarianpress.com

Wild Librarian Press
Santa Ana, California

Thank you for supporting a woman-owned independent press!

Contents

1	The Garden: Introduction to the Collection STACY RUSSO	

ESSAYS

7	A Year in Sissy's Garden EM BROUSSEAU
15	Origins and Ra(t)velations JIE TIAN
23	Babycakes Lives! Legacy of a Praying Mantis RENÉE FOLZENLOGEN
29	Mein Apfelbaum ALINA ZOLLFRANK
34	The Resurrected Garden HENRI BENSUSSEN
41	Perennial Life STEPHANI HEMNESS
46	Wish Fulfillment in a Garden CECILE MAZZUCCO-THAN
54	A Symphony of Nature: Rewilding My Garden in the Alps MICHAELA EMCH
59	My Gardens, My Children. My Children, My Gardens. CAROLYN DOEPKE BENNETT
65	A Reluctant Gardener: Lessons on Nature From My Dogs SASSAFRAS PATTERDALE
69	Ghost Garden CONNIE LEVESQUE
74	The Inspiration of Other Gardens SUELLEN COX
83	The Forest as Garden DEBORAH FLEMING
90	Ecce Homo [Sexual] Ad Hortus Conclusus OLUMAYOWA ANJOLAOLUWA WILLOUGHBY

95	Down and Dirty ELIZABETH BRULÉ FARRELL
100	Florilegium ROXANNE LIEN
105	William's Red Roses LYNDA MCKINNEY LAMBERT
110	Growing CAROL RAITT
117	The Charms of Botanical Gardens ELIZABETH KENNEDAY
124	About the Contributors
130	About the Editors

The Garden: Introduction to the Collection

Stacy Russo

I'M WRITING THIS ON a mid-October day in Southern California. In the early morning, it was cool, requiring a sweater and thick socks as I walked around the backyard of my wild garden to water the various plants and trees with my two dogs, Jack and Lily, tagging along. I have several fruit trees: pomegranate, grapefruit, lime, lemon, and orange. There are two pine trees I routinely trim and adorn with ornaments. A tall, wispy, and enchanting olive tree spreads out near my back fence close to old rosemary and rose bushes and vibrant bougainvillea. My garden has been a place of peace and playfulness for several rescue dogs including Joni, the first senior rescue with a white wolf-like coat who snorted and howled her magical songs while rubbing her large animal body against the plants. She used her nose and front paws to burrow in the dirt to hide bones and treats for later. It has been a few years since her passing, but Joni's spirit remains alive in my home and garden.

Now, in the afternoon of this October day, the sun is out and the air is warm and dry. I see people walking by in summer clothes from my living room window. Between my front door and the sidewalk is the wild garden of my front yard. It is lush and full of many wonders – varieties of sage, lavender, eucalyptus, ornamental grasses of different shades, Santa Barbara daisies, and a heavenly scented and robust spearmint plant. I removed some of the previous owner's lawn, but retained a nice-sized section. I'm glad I did. When my beloved, late dog Walter, another senior rescue, lost the use of his back legs from an injury and was undergoing rehabilitation, we spent time on the grass each day together, peacefully lying there on the soft bed beneath the sun while enjoying the scents and beauty of the garden. Some evenings, when the street and surrounding city were quiet, we did the same with the moonlight and stars.

When I think of my garden and the experiences I've had, several words come to mind: patience, learning, beauty, surprise, evolution. I can sit within it, almost completely still, and do nothing but look around in amazement. I delight in the birds making nests in the same strategic places each year. Some plants that appeared healthy and strong suddenly declined for an unknown reason and did not last the next season. Others that I believed were beyond help surprised me by showing new life and vibrancy that has continued for years. I am always learning. I remember the first time I lost track of time or any responsibilities and deadlines in the garden. I was simply sitting with the sun warming my face, watching the birds doing their thing.

It will soon be the 10th anniversary of my home. I never imagined I would have a house of my own, and certainly not a garden! Yet, living within the daily rhythm of a garden is not new to my body and soul. Half a century ago, when I was a child in 1970s Pennsylvania, I lived in a small house full of love with my parents and my brother, David. In the backyard, my dad tended a magnificent food garden. Apples, blueberries, peaches, strawberries, cherries, honeydew melons, watermelons, cantaloupes, squashes, cucumbers, green beans, zucchinis, lettuce, corn, Brussels sprouts, and varieties of potatoes and tomatoes are some gifts from his garden I remember. Near the midpoint of the garden and just a few feet from the strawberry patch I had some responsibility for, I often played within a grove of tall trees. In the shade of the canopy, hundreds of violets would bloom in the moist earth when the weather was warm. It was here, within this lush space, that my creativity and imagination ran free. I think of my dad's garden as the place where my creative life began.

My story of gardens is unique to my life, but profound memories of gardens – whether it be cultivating our own or visiting the creations of others – are something many of us share. If you are reading this book, I imagine gardens have been important in your life. In this inspiring collection, we get to read about the diverse experiences of gardens in the lives of contemporary writers. Similar to the seasons in a garden and the ups and downs shared by any gardener, these deeply personal essays range from joyful, transformative, resilient, and humorous to challenging, painful, and bittersweet. The garden mirrors our humanity and the cycles of our lives. Of course, we are not separate from nature, but part of it. These essays illuminate the multi-dimensional essence of gardens and all the wisdom to be found there.

Essays

A Year in Sissy's Garden

Em Brousseau

Winter

In February, I reached out to my manager, confirming my employment for the upcoming season. I was coming up on my second year of farming and assumed my hours would stay the same. But with budget cuts, I was down to thirty hours a week, and I knew I couldn't live off that. I also knew that I couldn't imagine living without farming. I live in a small area, and this is the only local farm. I was out of options, sinking into a depression, imagining quitting the career I loved for some data entry office job.

And then an email came through. I'm subscribed to an email list where farmers from all around my region can ask for advice, list job postings, sell produce, give away equipment, that sort of thing.

The life-changing subject line: *Older Woman Looking for Part Time Garden Help*.

It was posted on behalf of a woman in her seventies, who had a giant property and couldn't maintain it all on her own anymore. Tree habitats, marshland, foliage out front and back, and a very large garden. She just wanted someone for eight or so hours a week and paid $4 more an hour than my field crew wages. It was perfect – fifteen minutes away from me, filling the gaps in my schedule, paying *just* enough that I could afford another season at the farm I loved so deeply. With no hesitation, I applied.

Enough time had passed that I lost hope, until the woman – Sissy,

I learned, was her name – emailed me back to set up a time to tour her property. She called it Lucky Dog Farm, and it is one of the most beautiful places I've ever seen, even in winter.

Though it's chilly, Sissy takes me on a walk around her sizable land. We walk past the garden, fenced in and lined by prayer flags. She takes me around the wetlands that build the line between Lucky Dog Farm and the state forest. I learn of marsh marigolds and native orchids that bloom along the waterline in spring. Her tree habitats are encased in deer fencing, but through the wire I can see willows and pines, oaks and witch hazel. As we walk, she asks if I know anything about native plants, and I shamefully answer no. She asks if I'm familiar with the biodynamic calendar, with Eliot Coleman and his work on organic farming, native vs. invasive insects. The answer to every question is an increasingly embarrassing *no*. I need this job. I'm so afraid that my ignorance will be the thing that loses it for me. But my lack of knowledge doesn't seem to be a deterrent; in fact, as we walk, she begins to explain each concept, happy to teach me about these important things. I try to maintain eye contact as we meander through dried, brown grass and leafless trees.

The garden is messy. Some of the plants have been left to compost over the winter, each bed a graveyard. Decaying kale stocks, sticklike remains of sunflowers, all nourishing the soil in a decidedly un-pretty way. I'm used to barren fields and a sense of emptiness over the winter, but despite everything having died, it still feels alive here.

Despite the cold weather, the decaying garden, and my inexperience with every single important aspect of this job, I want the position and she seems like she might want to hire me. We round back to her driveway, and she takes down my phone number and lets me know that she'll be in contact shortly. A week later, she emails me. The job is mine. I feel ecstatic; that email is the beginning of one of the most influential years of my life, one of practical, spiritual, and emotional growth.

SPRING
When I return to Lucky Dog Farm a few months later, it's bursting

with life. Sissy has dozens of windchimes, all singing their mismatched songs together. The many bird boxes, scattered throughout open fields, are bustling with birds setting up their nests. She points out each new bird to me, explaining their names, their songs, the telltale signs to recognize them. These teachings are just the beginning of a season about to burst with practical knowledge.

The first thing she has me do is remove the plant refuse that has sat all winter. In soil just barely warmed by the increasingly closer spring sun, I pull out the stocks and stems I had seen on my tour. I dig inside the beds for sprawling root balls, which have fused with the ground after all these months. I'm not used to prepping beds in spring; when I go back to work, it's all been cleared. I find that there's something exciting about being part of the very beginning, knowing that these beds will soon be home to an array of crops and flowers and herbs.

I help her sow peas one day. I've never actually done that – there is some hand planting at the farm, but very minimal. Most of our planting is done on the back of a transplanter, a big tractor making divots into soil, us dropping plants into a rotating mechanism that sends them down into the ground. I recall starting farming, how excited I was to plant into soil. And I do enjoy it, but it wasn't exactly how I had hoped it would be. I wanted to get my hands dirty, become connected with the land and the plant as I carefully place a seed in or gently cover roots.

With Sissy, I get this. She teaches me to use a spade and carefully create a divot for seeds to go into. We kneel and place seeds carefully in the created tunnel, then cover them with soil and water. It's a simple process; it's routine to her, but it's important to me. A brief burst of emotion that I'd never experienced before washes over me, this overwhelming feeling of connection to the Earth and the nature around me. In the simple act of sowing peas, I found a seed of spirituality inside myself.

I had never considered if the mechanical nature of large-scale farms dulled my connection to nature; it always seemed like enough to me just to be surrounded by the beauty of it. One of my favorite places is our greenhouse, tables full of trays that are just barely showing adolescent green seedlings. Sissy's version of a greenhouse is her laundry room, equipped with steel shelves, grow lights, and a laundry sink that is constantly full of soil. One afternoon in spring, as I weed around her tree habitat, it began to rain. Typically, with inclement weather, Sissy will send me home. But we take shelter under her breezeway, and she listens, head tilted. The birds are still singing; she tells me that this is a sign the rain will pass soon. Rather than send me home or to work in the ongoing shower, she welcomes me into her laundry room-turned-greenhouse.

I am used to seeding. I love doing it, actually – being responsible for the beginning of life. Carefully placing seeds in soil, caring for them with the appropriate amounts of soil and water, warmth and spacing. Normally, I seed into plastic trays divided into different amounts of cells based on what is planted. I could do this ten thousand times over (which is good, as we seed a few thousand plants at a time) and still feel a childlike excitement when the seed finally germinates. I know the science behind it all but seeing that first pop of green fills me with an exuberant thrill.

Sissy does not seed the way I'm used to; in fact, she seeds in a way that I'd never seen before. She explains the process of *soil block* planting. Plastic trays, while efficient and convenient, are not the best for burgeoning plants. They cramp the plant; the seedlings become root-bound, and when it's time to put them into the ground you force them out with rounded pegs, damaging the roots. Here, the soil *becomes* the container. You compress the soaking wet soil into blocks, then deposit them onto the flat and place the seed in the center.

It's fun, if a little labor intensive – you really have to put your weight into it, or the soil blocks crumble as soon as you try to deposit them. But I learn of the plentiful benefits to this method. They create healthier seedlings because as soon as the roots reach the air, they stop growing until you place them in the ground. Instead of disturbing and tearing roots, the soil block is placed wholly into the dirt, where the roots begin growing once again.

Once I learn, it makes immediate sense – of course they will easily transplant, because it's as simple as placing soil into soil. It's entirely natural. And yet it never occurred to me how *unnatural* my usual seeding practice was. You can get so used to how you do something that you never wonder if there's a better way. Or you never learn that there are other ways at all. The beauty of working with Sissy was learning these other ways, to see what it truly felt like to take my time and appreciate a simple process.

I found myself entranced as I watched her systemically create blocks and drop them onto the flats, wondering what other systems of gardening I was missing out on by working on a big farm. In choosing to garden in a way that is respectful and supportive of the seeds we plant, we become more connected to them and their process. It's about what is best for the crops, not what's best for us. To garden is a gift. A chance to connect with nature. Soil blocking, to me, felt *right*, like this was the way it was meant to be done. It fed the flame I'd felt earlier, the feeling of gratitude and connection growing with each small lettuce seed.

Summer

As it grows hotter and weeds grow wilder, I spend much of my time at Sissy's weeding. I don't mind this; weeding is one of my favorite tasks. My hands in the dirt, pulling out the unwanted plants to give the others room to grow. Just mindless enough to be calming without becoming boring. I love seeing the garden beds cleaned up and picturesque after a job well done. This year, galinsoga seems to be the main offender. I spend hours with it, feeling beneath the dirt for the roots and pulling carefully. I fill bucket after bucket with the fuzzy green plant. There is plenty of room here for my mind to wander, and each afternoon my brain does what it does best: cycles through negative thoughts, my fears and worries about the constant *unknown* we experience.

This has happened all my life. I have learned different ways to quiet the thoughts momentarily: distract myself with music, repeat tired mantras, daydream until the thoughts get louder and shake me out of it. But as the summer wears on and the time alone builds, I learn a different way to calm down, to center myself.

The garden at this time of year is exceptionally gorgeous. I realize how truly breathtaking the scenery around me is. Sitting in the afternoon sun, I look around at the beauty that surrounds me. The beds of multicolored snapdragons, the recently bloomed sunflowers, tomatoes of various colors and sizes climbing up their trellises faster than I can comprehend. I see bumblebees happily pollinating the potatoes as monarchs dance around red zinnias. Though I know that my self-centric fears are unimportant, they feel so *big* in moments that they overtake me. But I see the life around me interact without so much as a care about my trivial fears. I am inconsequential, not in a woeful way but a joyful one. The world goes on around us: birds find food for their young, honeybees bring back pollen for their hives, vines climb up trellises taller and taller, producing their fruits whether or not anyone is here to pick them.

Weeding, after this, becomes meditative. Each day it becomes easier to calm my mind down as I look around and really *experience* what it is to be a part of these processes, to be just another piece of the busyness in the garden.

Fall

I bemoan the changing of the seasons. With every falling leaf and additional warm layer, I grieve another farming season coming to a close. Autumn has become complex for me; once my favorite season, it now signals an end to the work. The once-pleasant scent of cool air reminds me that my days outside are limited, that the long months of winter are approaching, keeping me inside, yearning to don my overalls and scrub dirt out from under my fingernails once again.

Fall is beautifully messy at Sissy's. The remains of plants past still linger in their beds. Each tree habitat is shedding, blowing leaves of various sizes and colors over the fields of native grasses. Ten-foot-tall tomato plants finally give up, falling out of their trellises. I watch as summer flowers meet their end, and marvel at the zinnias and nasturtium, still somehow going strong. Birds are abandoning their boxes, flying across the sky in perfect formation towards something warmer. She stops mowing and trimming, wanting to keep the grounds wild enough that they are beneficial to the creatures who stay over the winter.

While autumn has always felt like an ending, Sissy shows me that it is, instead, creating the foundation for spring's beautiful new beginnings. I rake the leaves from her front lawn and transport them to the native plant groupings that mark her property at every corner; soon they will decompose and form a mulch. Over the winter, this mulch will keep the weeds out, feed the roots nutrients so they stay strong, and create a home for hibernating pollinators. I am learning the perfectly cleaned up yards and fields that I'm used to are detrimental to our environment, trading necessary habitats for an aesthetically attractive landscape. I rip out decaying vines and flowers, placing them in the now overflowing compost piles. Come spring they'll line the soil around the new seedlings, their matter feeding the new plants in a cycle that's ever turning. Nothing goes to waste; nothing is ending, I realize. Nature is perpetually happening around us, even in the cold. The empty, lost feeling I have in the winter is egotistical: my time to be outdoors is paused, but there is still so much going on around us.

The day finally comes at the end of November. Sissy emails me partway through the week; it's too cold to continue our work. My year at Lucky Dog Farm has come to a close. Though the sadness that comes with putting my clippers and flannel shirts in the attic is still present, there is also a small seed of contentment germinating within, knowing that each piece of winter is setting the stage for another spring, bright and beautiful as ever.

A YEAR LATER

I email Sissy around the beginning of March, hoping she needs my help again. My time with her was truly spiritual; I left with a combination of practical skills, native species education, and an immense reverence for nature and our environment. I hope for another year of teachings about organic practices, of identifying native insects, of the meditative quietude that comes from being still and mindful in an idyllic, scenic garden.

Despite my hope, Sissy does not need me again. But the legacy of her knowledge lives on within me.

My partner and I learned of a community garden in our small town over the winter, hidden behind a park with only two dozen plots. And after inquiring, we found that there were plots available this year, ours if we wanted one. The zest for gardening I gained ignited through my body as we went through the process.

I order seeds, things we would never grow at the farm – things I grew with Sissy. Peas, both sweet and snap. Snapdragons and amaranth; rainbow carrots and lavender cauliflower. I draw up gardening plans the way I saw her do it, a page for each part of the growing season. Writing down what we'd seed and when, the best time for it to be transplanted, when it would be ready for harvest. And I make sure to put in companion plants, carefully considering what each crop would best benefit being next to. I'd never learned these things at work, but Sissy taught me how much *more* there is than simple efficiency and crop rotation to avoid pests. There is a greater relationship between plants than we ever truly consider, and it was with her that I learned to listen to what nature has done, to plant according to what is best for the crops, the soil, the insects, not in accordance to my convenience.

My time with Sissy was more impactful than I'd ever imagined. The wisdom and conscientiousness that she imparted onto me has long-lasting impacts. My time with her has made the planet a little bit better. There are a few more native plants improving the environment around me, bringing in our pollinators that are always facing competition from invasives. And I, too, am improved. From my time with her, I developed a spiritualistic and transcendental relationship with nature, creating a quietude within myself that had eluded me for so long. I am more intentional, more thoughtful, more caring because of what I'd learned and experienced with her. My gratitude for her, and for Lucky Dog Farm, will run deep into my veins like roots; I will carry this year with me for the rest of my life, and I will be grateful each day for it.

Origins and Ra(t)velations

Jie Tian

I GARDEN LIKE MY Chinese grandmother. I garden because of my grandmother. Rather, grandma gardens and farms while I just garden. In her garden there is food, flowers, and medicine. She tends them with the same diligence and care. Gardening endows her an independence that most women in the early twentieth century China do not have. After the death of her husband, she was able to raise her two daughters, my mother and my aunt, from a life on the land. I followed her around and watched her in the garden and in the field when I was a child, sheltered far away from the storms of the Cultural Revolution, in our ancestral homeland, the Chen's Plains, in the subtropical eastern Sichuan Province. She uses organic gardening methods, in collaboration with nature, weather, geography, and her relatives. I learned to feel for the land from her. I intuited from her how to care for and use plants for food and medicine.

When I start gardening in Southern California's Mediterranean climate, decades have passed since my childhood. I look for a home that would resemble the hilly contours of my childhood homeland, that would lean to the wild and release me into the open. And I am close. Situated on a hillside slope, my home is part of a community built in the 1980s in the then rural Yorba Linda. An example of how humans continuously etch an existence into the natural world. Facing the north, the south ridge of the Chino Hills State Park puts a halt to our penchant for growth and encroachment. Facing the south, the Santa Ana Mountain rises majestically in supreme silence near the horizon. The coastal range gradually undulates toward the west where the ocean is. Below the mountain and the hills, the Santa Ana River, sometimes dried and stalled, sometimes flows unhurriedly to the sea, encased in concrete. The air from the Pacific and the high desert cross paths here, through the Santa Ana Canyon, carrying ocean breeze and scorching winds from opposite directions, in alternating seasons of drought and wet weather – if we are lucky to have rain in the winter season. The 91 Freeway cuts through the canyon, severing an otherwise harmoniously connected natural terrain.

In this web of geography, I make my garden. My garden has lived for a long time in my mind, before I sowed the first seed. There are memories of my homeland and my grandmother. There are inspirations from my poetry ancestors who farm, garden, or make—Emily Dickinson, Wendell Berry, Stanley Kunitz, Du Fu, Xue Tao. There is grief and gratitude to the land and to Native American ancestors— the Tongva, Luiseño, and Juaneño people—who relied on this land for their way of life for thousands of years before colonization and their erasure and forced removal. I want to experience a sense of self-reliance, to live a kinder life, closer to the earth, closer to the spirits, by choosing to garden. I want to create a permaculture garden that models the forest ecology, with tiers and layers covering the ground, in between, and reaching into the sky. Most of all, my garden will honor the indigenous wisdom that regards the land and all beings as sacred and related. My garden will be a small habitat that welcomes "all my relations."

The previous owner, Jean, keeps the garden efficient and minimalist. A small greenish-brownish lawn as the front yard, a few straggly geraniums scatter along the side yard, one colony of kalanchoe below the entrance patio, two clumps of star jasmine covering the backyard slope. A replica of our Southern California suburban landscape. Everywhere else, reddish volcanic gravel of various sizes covers the ground, six inches deep. I uncover the depth of the amendment much later, one spring afternoon when I begin to dig into the soil. I am also digging into native land, formed over eighteen million years ago as the result of the last tectonic shift, and for thousands of years nourished native people, until Spanish colonization, and later the American Westward Expansion and invasion. This recent suburban development scrapes off native vegetation, yet the land remains "wild" and largely uncultivated, with Jean as the first owner of this parcel.

I sense the magnitude of my choice, wanting to make a garden, to grow food and medicine, to create a habitat, to simulate an ecology. I would break the monotony of a massive landscape. I preserve Jean's plants, keeping some and giving away the rest. I have the front lawn removed and invite in trees and native plants: artemisia californica, a variety of native sage, wooly blue curls, native fuchsia, and mint. The side yard is reenacted as a sort of an apothecary, with herbs, a variety of roses, and grandma's daylilies, honeysuckle, and hollyhocks—after much investigation into whether roses are a sustainable choice, or whether they would demand too much water. On the backyard slope, I plant more trees, building the structure of a forest, however small it is. Between and under the trees is my experimental territory for vegetables, herbs, and flowers, carrying on grandma's agrarian tradition. In Sichuan, we farm, we make the land fertile and sing—at least we used to. And as the wise saying goes: It would take one hundred years to build a rich soil structure. I am taking my first step here. I am still digging out gravel whenever I wish to reuse another inch of land.

My garden will not be neat and orderly as a picture-perfect suburban garden. I want this small parcel of land to echo the nearby hills in form and composition, and to take after a forest ecology that also provides sustenance for birds, bees, insects, and animals. Knowing the importance of freedom, I say to myself, *everyone is welcome, everyone is free to come and go.* And indeed, they come—lizards, rabbits, squirrels, racoons, honeybees, bumble bees, butterflies, dragonflies, ladybugs, aphids, hummingbirds, wren, gnat catcher, bluebirds, mockingbirds, doves, quail, crows, roadrunner, snakes, and rattlesnakes. And certainly, there are many more visitors and inhabitants than I know, than I can see or name. Indeed, with or without my knowing, they also go at their own timing and volition. Their visitations fill my garden with surprise, delight, astonishment, sometimes fear and anxiety.

Yet none of these beings have made an impression, invited a prolonged interaction, or evoked a range of emotions that would rival the mice and rats. Why would I not also have included them as part of my habitat? Clearly, they are not on my mind or on my list, when I sing praise of "all my relations"—despite my expansive outlook and ecological consciousness. Subconsciously, I could be discounting them from my garden or any garden. And they are here, this living moment, under my roof, underground, in my garden. They are here, holding permanent residency. They are also there, primordial as time, in our collective memory, predating recorded human history, in the *Book of Songs,* the first collection of Chinese poetry, dated five thousand years ago. Their presence looms large in the folk poem, *Giant Rat*. I would chant the poem from my childhood textbook. They haunt my childhood. The poem's strong cadence, rhythm, refrain and repetition immortalizes the rat—

> Giant Rat Giant Rat, don't eat my millet
> . . .
> Giant Rat Giant Rat, don't eat my wheat
> . . .
> Giant Rat Giant Rat, don't eat my seedling
> . . .

And there is much more to the poem, as it is taught to children. The accusations of the rat allude to the exploitative and destructive behaviors of the imperial ruling class. The poem expresses common people's desire for a peaceful and egalitarian society, and their own slice of an (unattainable) paradise.

When I first see mice in my garden, with my childhood fear gone, I am amused, even elated. Why wouldn't I be? They scurry by, light as air, swift as a swallow. They are small, alert, and attractive. I can never track their activities or whereabouts among the bushes and vegetation, front and back, up and down the garden tiers. They are an illusory phantom intelligence, an enchanting yet fleeting companion to a solitary gardener who works in silence, going about her routine: cutting back old growth, sowing seeds, watering. The few times when I catch them eating in my garden, I praise their neatness, small appetite, restraint, and good taste. How can I fault a well-groomed, smoothly coated gray-black fellow, seeking shelter from sultry summer heat under a bush, nibbling on the fallen yellow petals of the Poet's Wife rose? How can I not be astonished when I see an early riser on a misty spring morning straddling on the head of a stalk of kale, next to a blooming pink yarrow, munching, munching. What a beautiful setting and a crisp breakfast. I cannot help but compose Haiku to commemorate our encounter—

of mice and woman—
quietly they move dawn to dusk
one tending one munching

of mice and woman
they eat from the same bounty
—autumn reverie

Then they come, the Giant Rats. They are different from mice. Bigger, huskier, carrying great force and speed, they would burst onto the scent and thump into action. I sense an urgency in their movement and a menace. These nocturnal creatures would descend in the guise of night and rapidly dispatch themselves into the garden. I learn about their behavior by registering loss. The first lily buds of the season thrust on the sidewalk. Tomatoes gnawed open, hanging on the vine like half broken red moons. Piles of fava beans and pods skillfully shred into thin strings. Sweet potatoes dug out of the ground and gnawed with tooth marks. One by one, all the peaches on a young tree are gone. They cut off the main stem of the pole bean when the vine has climbed up high. They pluck out the flowering snow pea. They peel the bark off the miju mandarin tree—I watch the tree slowly die in three years.

It is one thing to eat from the garden. It is another thing to kill. I cannot not feel, walking the garden grounds, spring through summer into fall. Grief. Helplessness. Sometimes shame. Sometimes rage. These could be instinctual and maternal feelings. These are elemental feelings. I am deprived of the fruits of my labor. I can't protect the beings that I have invited to my garden. In some misty mornings, I am gray like a spider web hung with cold dew, grief woven into my veins. I grieve for the life unlived, unfulfilled. What to do, and what can I do? How can I tell the rats not to kill?

A friend tells me the story of a Buddhist gardener. She makes a separate garden, in the opposite direction from her own, for insects and animals. She would chant to them, and they would know to go to their own plot and leave her garden alone. Chants or otherwise, most suburbanites and farmers of our time rely on pest control companies. They would cite the cardinal crimes of the rodent species and extol their own expertise, technique, and technology. Their strategy is elimination and removal. This strategy is not new. It is part of the American Westward Expansion. In *Coyote America,* historian Dan Flores details the brutal, systematic, professional killing of coyotes and rodents in the nineteenth-and-early-twentieth century North America. Through legislation, government funding, manufacturing of traps and poisons, and establishing agencies such as the "Division of Predatory Animal and Rodent Control (PARC)," America heralds wildlife killing in order to make way for farmers and other landowners who would settle the frontier land. History still repeats itself, now in suburban homes and gardens.

Haunted, I am also acutely intrigued by the giant rats. If I resort to the extermination of a pest control company, I would be less of a participant in the struggle and experience. In my mind is also my grandmother's kind gardening practice. I feel an urge to learn, to investigate, firsthand. This urge revives me. Many evenings in the spring and summer, I would go into the dark and wait. I would sit under the grapevine on the upper patio, holding my breath. I would wait, not knowing what to expect, not without fear. I wave away flying moths and mosquitoes. I hear owls hooting in the east, where the tall trees are, on land uninhabited by us humans. I see the moon rise in the west, forlorn and calm. City lights on the Anaheim hills blink in languid intervals like small sea anemones.

One spring evening, while not really looking, I see them. Rapid moving bodies. Long tails. Racing on the fence, as pearlescent light gives way to dark. Instantly they descend. Quickly I lose sight of them, but I hear them, in the lower tier. Rustling in leaves. Bumping on things. Moving here and there. Timid yet ravishing. Night is a scepter. Night is not my domain. I garden, I want to live closer to the earth, but I do not—not close enough, in comparison with them. They burrow on the earth. They live closer to the earth. I would spend many more nights outside, through the seasons, sensing their secretive and animated movements. Often, sleep drags me indoors, long before they conclude their nocturnal activities.

And I would read all I can about them. Blogs, discussion forums, websites, folklores, research studies. Most of all, the rats reveal themselves to me, through the traces they leave behind the night before. I would discover them in my early morning walks. As I walk, in the gray of the morning, I often hear the poet, Dylan Thomas: *Rage, rage against the dying of the light.* Rage, hand in hand with helplessness. Yet there is gain. There is an opening of the mind, a new bravery, peace and comfort with the dark, the unknown—after I venture out, even if it is the dark and unknown in my own backyard. I feel a closer connection with night and dark. I feel the pulse of night, the breath of the earth. More than ever, a oneness. A concept which I intellectualize often, but not feeling in an experiential, sensory, or bodily way. The longer I remain in darkness, the more light I see. In darkness, there is much light to be perceived. I wonder if death is also darkness and light in one. My deeply buried, long-lodged fear of death seems to gradually dissolve into the vast night sphere.

After rage and grief flow out of my body, I resort to reason. I seek understanding. What is true ecology? Do rats have a place in this ecology? When does ownership begin? Why does property matter? Do the harvests of my garden belong to me alone? Why do I drive a hard wedge between them and me? What justice is there in my claim to the entirety of the fruits of my labor? Why can't I let go? What can't I let go? How would the rest of creation regard us humans when we cut down forests, hunt out animals, pollute land, water, air, ocean, and the atmosphere? What if my garden is a small part of a vast forest and there is an abundance of food and shelter for every living being? Would I want to oust the rats then? My questions are tangled and connected, like the web that we live in and cannot untangle. Again and again, I resort to Native American wisdom to enlarge my worldview. In *Becoming Kin: An Indigenous Call to Unforgetting the Past and Reimagining the Future,* Patty Krawec, an Anishinaabe and Ukrainian writer from Lac Seul First Nation, speaks of *overlapping claims* to the places we live. She asserts that plants and animals also have claims.

And I am not quite awake to the claims of certain animals, even as I set out to recreate a small habitat, to welcome "all my relations." I have a limited notion of ecology. My choices are selective and exclusive, and I have my personal favorites. In the end I come to see: It is the unwelcome guests, rats in particular, that turn out to be my great teachers. They compel me to stop in my tracks, and pause, to examine their revelations. They know the timing and progression of growth better than I. They are drawn to what I am drawn to in the garden. I admire their facility, economy, and adventurous spirit. They explore with an unmatchable viscera and physicality. They ravish and relish the dark and the unknown. They also reveal beauty that I would otherwise miss. After all, we have co-existed since *The Book of Songs,* since time immemorial. And so will we continue. This is a good education for any gardener. Even with grief, I sing and marvel at their teachings: Ra(t)velations.

Babycakes Lives! Legacy of a Praying Mantis

Renée Folzenlogen

IT WAS A DARK and stormy night. A strong rain pounded the dark earth of the little side garden. The indifferent wind ruffled the spiky, neglected branches of the butterfly bush. It wanted a trim, but the absentminded gardener was inside the house drinking a cup of hot tea. Moisture trickled down the leggy wood, soaking into the brittle cover of leaves and scrappy grasses. Underneath, nestled in the rich dark earth, rested peacefully one black rabbit named Hot Fudge, two parakeets called Cloud and Mulan, and Striker, the garden snake, fallen victim to an unexpectedly lethal encounter with a toxic, slimy garden slug. No matter the manner of their deaths, all the pets were laid to rest in old shoeboxes, wrapped lovingly in cast-off tissue paper, and honored with bouquets of dried flowers, tied with reused gift ribbon. Each had words said over them by a mother and her gathering of three small children. The years passed, the children grew, left home, fell in and out of love, phoned home, or didn't, and only occasionally gave a thought to the little black rabbit, the downy feathered flashes of wings, and the serpentine companion who have each gone the way of all things. The children's mother remained. She began to dig, and to plant, and to water.

By the first summer of the global pandemic of 2020, the southeast corner of this tiny slice of pie garden in suburban New Jersey was taking shape. Haphazard in design, inhabitants were acquired at an alarming rate, without much forethought, the way one might adopt a stray kitten in need of shelter. A tiny maple was planted here, in the corner next to the neighbor's fence, a miniature ginkgo tucked over there, between the white stucco garage and the creeping juniper, so old and big that we call it our "Badger" and named it Gandalf. Lavender, sage, bleeding heart, blazing orange butterfly weed, wild mint, and plump stonecrop the color of milky jade. Pachysandra threatened to take over and had to be periodically culled. Herbaceous peonies kept a steady flow of ants happy, slurping the sticky juices. The growing Eden hosted a fine parade of bumble bees, honey bees, hummingbirds, moths, tiger swallowtails, and cabbage whites. Any beneficial protein from the pet cemetery was long ago absorbed into the hearty, neglected butterfly bush.

It was about this time of heightened blooming, with the sun high in the midsummer sky when the infatuation began. What was first seeded as pure curiosity, quickly sprouted into admiration, settled into surprising affection, and a deep need for connection with one particular insect. I found myself drowning heart deep in feelings of sincere attachment for one strange and alien creature, a female praying mantis, christened by me, as Babycakes. Don't ask me why. Maybe the name was born from a need to quell my fears of her terrible mandible and cold hearted, calculating gaze. When I made her acquaintance, Babycakes was a generous four and three quarters inches in length, still as stone, and fast as lightning. I never loved a bug so much in all my years, and never will again. You can be sure of that. My affection was a one-way street. 'Til the day she died, Babycakes never once wasted a bit of her love on me. She was a monster, and I was her minion, planting and tending the orange-eye butterfly bush that became her summer home, the eventual site that sheltered her egg sac, and the birthplace of her progeny.

I came to know her daily routine. When the sun was high, you'd find her on those outer, uppermost branches of the untrimmed bush, hanging winsomely, head first, raptorial legs folded, and at the ready. Once or twice I caught Babycakes lazing upside down, letting those leggy weapons relaxed and open, airing out her armpits in the breeze. A mature Mrs. Robinson napping by the swimming pool waiting for the afternoon snack to be served by a lanky young lover who would later lose his head.

Babycakes was a thing of beauty, at least to me. I'd step out in between meetings with a cup of hot tea, and squat, peering at her as closely as she'd permit. Once, our gazes locked, and a chill ran through me. It was I who took half a step backwards, sucking in my breath as quietly as I could, trying to appear nonchalant, until she lost interest and went back to surveilling the path of a poor, unsuspecting bee. Her front legs reached out for the mid-air snatch, a kind of Hail Mary pass, and I cheered inside when she made contact – *Way to go, Babycakes*! She tore at the bee's abdomen. Silence fell. Oblivious to the flailing legs of her still living prey, Lady Mantid ripped off its head with a satisfying crunch, reminiscent of breakfasting on a bowl of Special K. *Behold!* The juicy dripping golden guts of bumblebee – there perched Babycakes, like a medieval lord with a goblet of mead, letting the honey dribble from her lips.

I'm convinced this creature made me smarter, wiser, and more patient. Watching Babycakes, the stillness in me only deepened, but my darling monster, she sure knew how to move. I learned that praying mantises are exceptional at leaping, pouncing, and swirling in midair. Advancing towards a target, their heads can swivel 180 degrees, using stereoscopic vision to land with surgical precision. Included in her repertoire is a sequence of movements I call the *Mantis Amble*: tenderly repositioning one slender leg at a time, feeling along the surface with her tippy toes, body imperceptibly rocking, gaining purchase against the side of the garage. Delicate and deadly, she commanded my – no – *her* little Eden. She was a perfect pandemic companion, untouched by the terror of global disease, rising social unrest, and loneliness.

The feverish dahlias bloomed late and slow, opening with a slow burn, then opening more, more, more! Like a dragon with a million tongues, sticking them all out at once – *this is how I am – take it or leave it*. The goldfinch, a flying flash of melted butter, snacked on lavender – *if you catch sight of me, mere human, you are blessed*. Mourning doves cooed at dawn and dusk, nesting. Hungry rabbits made the precious stonecrop disappear. Babycakes didn't care one whit. She was immersed in her own existential struggle and she was on top. As many bees as she caught, she missed countless others. Yet the Mistress persisted. She fattened. She molted. Grew heavy and prepared. Soon, I adopted my own mantra: *When in doubt, go to the garden.* I'd learn something there, dreaming backwards and forwards in time, lost inside the waving forest of a single butterfly bush, tracking the movement and stillness of Babycakes.

Summer waned and I dreaded the thought of Babycakes going the way of all things, sharing the fate of Striker, Fudge, Cloud, and Mulan. I'd said goodbye to so many. And the thought of not seeing that nuance of green hidden amidst the leaves, the beguiling navette-shaped wings, that cocked and swiveling head, ready to pounce – she stirred me, she did, adventure was packed in that taut little form, and I wasn't ready to say goodbye. Until I found the egg sac, delicately suspended from a branch of our Russian sage plant, like a gnarly old walnut, swollen and muddy gray. Paper thin armor guarding hundreds of tiny eggs within.

Waiting. Waiting. Waiting.

My husband Tim and I speculated about the unmarked day that Babycakes passed into the great beyond. After some debate, we concluded that she was too great in spirit, too long in the tooth, and too cunning and tough of flesh to fall prey to a fellow predator.

"I could see a young and untried Babycakes being snatched up by a bird or a bat, but not after all she's been through. She was a warrior."

We concluded that Babycakes had succumbed to the cold of the approaching winter, having passed quietly alongside the garden debris from hypothermia.

"Probably after a brief bout of delirium," added Tim, softly dropping his head to one side, letting his eyes roll back, then closing them in finality to demonstrate the imagined death mask of our beloved praying mantis legend.

"She's grass now," he said, putting a period on the matter.

I'd been keeping tabs on the egg sac since Babycakes' demise. My vigilance consisted of stepping out during the cold winter months just to see if it was still there. Poking it now and then with my finger. Wondering how anything could still be alive in that shriveled up old husk. Like the Matriarch, it persisted. Then spring arrived, and an army of ants, bored with the peony's sweetness, gnawed open a tiny hole in the papery shell. Outrage ensued! I flew into action, and transplanted it, still precariously tethered on its branch of sage to one spiky arm of the still unclipped butterfly bush. Secured it with a prayer and a wish and a cast-off gift ribbon. Hidden in the greenery, it remained unassaulted as the spring rains fell and the temperatures rose.

On that momentous day of May 14, 2021, I was out of step with everything. Slow to rise and late to breakfast. I spilled coffee on my shirt, changed into a wrinkled one, had to take it off again and iron it. My damp, unruly hair was a mass of vines, refusing to be tamed. When I finally made it out the door, I realized I'd forgotten the keys and locked myself out of car and home. Choking back a sob of anxiety, I did the only sensible thing and surrendered. I plopped my bag at the base of the honeysuckle, allowing its high-pitched, scented sweetness to waft over my agitation. As I gave way to my usual inspection of blooms in the side garden, my eyes lit upon Babycake's egg sac. There, amidst the waving leaves of the butterfly bush, I spied something new, something strange, a kind of magic.

At first I couldn't make any sense of it. The bottom edge of the weathered old sac began to spit out a golden clump of strings, transparent strands tipped with what appeared to be ghostly eyes. Like the soft plop from a newborn's butt, this quivering lump oozed downwards, slow, steady, and sloth-like. One of the strands gave a vertical shake and shuddered away, a fully formed miniature mantis, landing safe and sound, on the leaf below, its newly made cradle of green. Just above, another creature separated from the golden mass, stretching tiny, threadlike arms, its head now defined from its thorax. The newly freed aerialist rotated its body fully, and then contracted upwards, like an acrobat you might see at the circus; that "daring young man on the flying trapeze," twirling headfirst, arms and legs moving in graceful arabesque patterns while stealing hearts in the audience. The mantis babies were no less magnificent.

"Hey, hello there, I knew your mother, little ones," I found myself whispering.

My voice grew louder, deeper.

"She was fierce. You'll be fine."

She lives! my battered old heart cried.

I thought those morning missteps were in my way, slowing me down from where I needed to be. Instead, they were nudging me out of my own way, benevolent sheepdogs herding me towards the Miracle in the Butterfly Bush, the place I truly wanted to be. Maybe it was the soul of Babycakes' ghost, totem animal extraordinaire. Indulge me on this. You see, at times, I like to think that I am watched over by the angels of my father, my mother, my sister, my pet rabbit Fudge, and now, it seems, by the fierce and fidele praying mantis called Babycakes. So, little mantises, I christen thee, Romulus and Remus, Rory and Boris, Clive and Helene, Abelard and Heloise, and so on and so forth, to the tune of 300. Which of you will survive, and what happens next? A soft and steady rain begins to fall. The butterfly bush is again in want of a trim. The gardener retreats inside the house for a hot cup of tea.

Mein Apfelbaum

Alina Zollfrank

IN ONE, ONLY ONE, black-and-white photo of my middle-school years, I appear content, radiant almost. Wrapped in my puffy winter jacket, I hang from an aging tree, arms and legs wrapped sloth-like around an expansive lower branch, heels anchored in a perfectly molded groove where the stem forks to form the crown. My head is tossed back, my neck exposed, and I beam at the camera. Even as a sullen, imbalanced teenager who often withdrew from others, I knew that every human deserves a special place in nature to connect with the outside world and honor what's ancestrally, culturally still inside of us. A single plant can generate an indelible mark on our psyche. In my case, this apple tree of undefined variety was it.

Under a gabled roof, our thick-walled stone home huddles into the nook of an unpaved dead-end street named "Stork's Nest." Once a bare-bones garden bungalow, presumably erected in the early 1920s, it was clumsily expanded, piecemeal-style, during and right after World War II. My parents moved in when I was still wearing diapers. Whenever I try to conjure memories of the building now – a slightly strenuous task because I haven't been back home, as I continue to call it, in a baker's dozen years – a tree, *the* tree, emerges crisply in the back, causing the actual building to pale in the foreground. Planted by an earlier generation and later expertly tended by my Opa and my Papa – both talented hobby gardeners – the old apple set the tone for long childhood days, teenage dreams, and adulthood choices. I grew up under and in this metaphor for belonging.

"Mein Apfelbaum" – my apple tree – acted as focal point of the backyard, fenced in by tall wooden slats streetside, concrete walls to the left and right, and roaming industrial railway tracks behind. I learned that the small plot surrounding the whitewashed, red-shingled, be-chimneyed home signified sustenance for generations before my time. When I was in preschool and bravely descended the steep, curling stone stairs into the musty basement, dusty remnants of great-aunts' and uncles' efforts sat on custom-built wooden shelves and bore labels handwritten by ancestors I had never met. I'd visit jarred ghosts with a flashlight; the sole cellar bulb jutting from the wall barely showed outlines of shapes. This was my descent into yesterday. Some glass containers housed cherries in juice, transformed to a russet, congealed mess with fuzzy floaters. There were pear chunks, transparent in their age and wobbling in liquid. And then there was applesauce in ancient glass jars. If I'd had the courage to lift them off the shelf, I would have lacked the muscle strength to twist the lids open. Without someone telling me so, I was aware that the apples in this – likely inedible – applesauce had come from one of the oldest trees on the lot, the one that prominently took the stage facing our low kitchen window, the one that dwarfed the house and garden.

Oddly, I don't remember apple blossoms, apple growth, or apple harvest. I do remember my dad lifting me up so I could hang from trusty branches on clear, fresh days. A slight child with muscular deficits, I needed a boost to get into the tree and a reliable helping hand to come back down. My bones felt brittle, my joints jiggly. Maybe this was fear raising her prominent voice as she often did, or maybe I had an honest handle on what my physique could and couldn't do.

One glorious day, though – and I don't recall how old I nor what season it was – I arrived strong, tall, and adept enough to hoist myself up on my own. The tree, my only witness for this sudden feat, invited courage. The lowest branch had recently been sawed off. My dad, following in my grandfather's wise footsteps, had covered the knobby cut with a thin layer of cement to prevent pest invasion. From now on, I could firmly lodge the arch of my foot across this little ledge – a wound moulded for eternity – then shove off the ground with my other set of toes and, defying gravity, launch my arms upward until they snatched the rough, old bark. The tree was there for me. Huffily, I'd pull myself higher and swing my other leg across the central part of the stem, the part I liked to think of as a division of roads because from there, large branches stretched into all directions, as if invisible paths extended out into possibilities.

On days like the one in the old photograph, I'd bundle up, climb into my perch, and snatch a blurry glimpse at the distant town beyond our neighbor's yard, past the train tracks behind the strawberry planter, our evergreen hedges, and over flat garage roofs. Bare branches would hold me as long as I could hold out, and no leaves impeded my view. The sky opened her fresh arms above me and turned antithesis to the fruity remains and lore of ancestors in our dank basement. This was my ascent into tomorrow. This was my place. No one else fit here.

I could look at my childhood home from this distance, squint to change perspective, and imagine I was Gulliver in a land of littles. Sometimes, I became Nils Holgersson and joined noisy flocks of wild geese overhead on their travels to and from Sweden. Other days, I'd drag a jump rope up with me and let it dangle from the tree, like Rapunzel about to be rescued. But a damsel in distress I was not. I was a lonely, sickly child, and when I felt absolutely sure no one was looking, I'd rest my hands against the bark of the tree and have a profound conversation with it. Decades have since passed and erased my memory of the details of such chats, but I suspect there were whispers, serious confessions, and also mutual comfort. Young skin pressed against craggy bark, we might have silently exchanged philosophical thoughts on the meaning of life, what bravery was, and whether belonging meant rooting into the ground, being scattered across a meadow, or placing feet wherever the heart felt like landing. On my confident days, like the one in the photo, I'd raise my hips up from this seat and my voice into the sky and try to convince the wind to take me on a journey. I craved elsewhere. The tree seemed like the ideal lift-off spot and I knew, I knew, I could fly if I just believed hard enough. If I let the blackbirds overhead teach me, and if I trusted the wind to keep me aloft and guide me where I was meant to go, I'd soar.

Eventually, inevitably, hunger would demand descent. I'd sneak into the cold storage room and forage for hidden stashes of Zwieback, butter cookies, marble cake, and soft, fragrant apples from last season. Or I might flip the hundred-year-old black light switch that required an assertive flick of my wrist and, with a satisfying thwack, would create minor illumination so I could carefully come to the dim dungeon and contemplate the spiderweb-covered jars of fruit preserves that had been patiently slumbering beneath the earth for generations. If I paid attention, they murmured stories of famine and resilience, of busy hands and rich harvests, of careful planning and ancestral wisdom.

Today I watch Queen Cox and Elstar blossoms tease out a slow opening for the hovering Mason bees. My memory, as I listen to the buzz, becomes murky again, but I recall reading somewhere that scientists discovered a tree can remember its childhood. I devour a late Opal apple from an organic farm in Eastern Washington and cannot help but wonder if its seeds contain some sort of generational memory, and whether it would share those stories with other apple seeds and trees. My childhood tree's physical presence is now gone; I only have a vague inkling of my reaction when I saw the chopped stump in the middle of my parents' meadow. Growing up in a garden came with lessons about change as a constant, and acceptance as an adaptive mechanism.

Decades ago, I crossed the wide ocean seated behind the wings of planes and landed in a new place. My old tree in the Storchennest garden, maybe not surprisingly, seeded memories that affected my adult choices. I picked this home in the Pacific Northwest before birthing my babies because the dense lot showed gardening potential. The house is an ongoing, at times frustrating, project, but when I compare photos of the garden from twenty years ago to today, I know my coming-of-age apple tree's legacy lives on in my actions. I have planted ten apples on this small lot and only lost one (I mourned it, deeply). My children climbed the bold Gravenstein while *it* was little while *they* were little; now, that giant has outpaced them and all the dwarf-sized trees in its vicinity. I talk to my apple trees when I want to coax fragrant blossoms from pink buds or when I'm concerned that leaves and fruit are not coping well with the increasingly frequent wildfire smoke. Even during the years when the trees refuse to bud or when they drop their fruit prematurely, I have a peaceful chat with them. Some days might find me, aged palm flattened against warm bark, listening to the trees' voices and silently imploring them to ground me in this place, with their roots, because mine have yet to grow. I'm *that* odd bird in the neighborhood, the one who gifts pounds and pounds of apples every harvest season to neighbors and communal share spots and who cooks applesauce with devotion.

And while I don't climb up anymore to look across the big, wide world, or dream of stretching wide wings into the breeze, I've found that rolling out my yoga mat and peering up into apple trees from a new vantage point can induce a sense of bizarre, almost dizzying, happiness.

I might invoke memories of my ancestors with their competent arms full of apples, their hands busily canning fruit, their grateful noses immersed in apple blossoms. I might grin; I might hum; I might ask the Canadian geese overhead, "How's it going?" and "Where are you traveling?" I am, contentedly, an overgrown kid who belongs to the canopy.

The Resurrected Garden

Henri Bensussen

THE SUMMER OF 1999 I celebrated my 62nd birthday by retiring from a stressful job. My partner Kim and I would soon escape Silicon Valley and the corporate world by moving to Fort Bragg on California's Mendocino Coast, a lumber and fishing town of about seven thousand souls on the edge of the Pacific. Three years before I'd been able to buy a run-down house surrounded by almost half an acre of bleached grass on a narrow one-way street at the town's south end, about a mile east of the ocean. I'd been sustained during those pre-retirement years by mentally planning how to landscape this half acre. I'd created three gardens during my life, all of which I'd had to leave. This one would be my last and largest. I didn't want to think of ever giving it up. I'd read of a woman who had died in her garden, and that sounded like a perfect ending for me as well.

Due to the high-water table, the house, built in the 1920s, was held up on 30-inch high, 8-inch square redwood posts. A tough Cécile Brünner rose grew along the weathered picket fence in front. Some fruit trees grew in back. Redwoods, two cottonwoods, pines and maples followed the west and north side fences, fronted by rampant blackberries. In a back corner was a shallow well and small well house. When we moved there in 1999, carpenters were still making final changes on our now renovated house and a new garage.

Kim enjoyed gardens but not the labor and planning of them, which was my passion and which I was going to fully indulge. Digging holes for plants was a different challenge. The house was near the street, on the southern half of our deep lot. The fruit trees that grew behind the house were apple, pear, plums, and apricot. The other half of the lot was either hard-packed, road-base gravel from a former driveway or three inches of soil over iron oxide hardpan and marine pebbles. Greywacke, a muddy, gray shale that became wet clay in winter, lay under that, another sign of a high-water table. Former owners had added odd amendments picked up from building sites. Invariably, as I dug into the soil, my shovel hit chunks of asphalt, cement paving, old bricks, or compacted clay rocks that in some cases were the size and weight of boulders.

Deer showed up in the fall, a doe with a fawn, a buck with two-pronged antlers. We put in fences and gates to save the heritage roses I was planting. Mounds of dirt in spring showed the presence of moles. Holes gave evidence of voles, a kind of meadow mouse. Like small gophers, they fed on plant roots. I tried a variety of barriers to protect the plants by burying them in pots or surrounding the roots with wire. A striped garden snake lived under an old brush pile and its progeny would eventually spread into the new flower beds I was constructing. More snakes meant less voles. Early in spring mornings little brown cottontail rabbits nibbled at grass near the gravel driveway. A large brown bat flew above the back garden in the early evenings, and once we saw an opossum on the back fence.

Heaps of compost and soil were delivered, and I shoveled it on top of the former hard-packed rock driveway to provide more space for flower beds. The far back area on the west, extending around to the north side, became my forest stand-in, with its redwoods, pines, cottonwoods, large maples, and new tall-growing shrubs and the climbing rose I added.

Throughout the garden I raked new paths to set off different spaces, forming rooms like the formal gardens I'd seen in English gardens. I'd weed these paths, put down a thick layer of newspaper or cardboard, and top it off with bark, leaves, the detritus of fall and the shearings of spring. I was always on the lookout, as I drove up and down the coast's many side roads, for free chopped up tree trimmings. My small pickup truck got a lot of use on these forays.

The ever-growing blackberry patch fronted the line of redwoods and two cottonwoods that grew along the back fence. As I cut back the berry patch I'd expose old fire circles containing pieces of foil, plastic debris, broken bottles, piles of ancient brush, roofing shingles, chicken wire, a couple of baseballs. With the blackberries and trash gone I planted abutilons, new irises, a collection of rose bushes, and a grove of Japanese maples.

We made a pond with a small fountain and a water lily using a Japanese, 30-inch diameter, 28-inch deep, clay pot, placing it close to the back deck. Behind it I planted a flowering crabapple. The well house was converted into a potting and tool shed, and a planter box constructed for seasonal vegetables or flowers. This box, plus pavers for a patio floor, a couple of garden chairs, and a tall, blue stone birdbath, became a private space within the larger garden. I liked to sit there with a book, enclosed on two sides by an arbor and an ell of lath fencing, and facing the abutilons and redwoods.

Sara Stein, in *Noah's Garden: Restoring the Ecology of Our Own Backyards*, wrote that even in suburbia one could return to a natural world. While land couldn't be restored completely to its primeval state, a new landscape could be created and encouraged to revert to a natural, balanced ecosystem of wildness. She called this a "new esthetic, . . . [a] distillation of the larger landscape." More than distilling a landscape, I was digging up its ancient bones, forming a personal retreat for the survivors of neglect. Bringing a landscape to life brought energy and well-being, as if we were plants, too.

Kim and I joined the Garden Club and the Friends of the Mendocino Coast Botanical Gardens, where I also became a master gardener. I joined the Rhododendron Club, and thus acquired thirty rhodies over the years, usually at the meetings; many members were growing them for sale. We volunteered at the Botanical Gardens and helped with the annual fund-raising events. Its annual sales provided a lot more plants for my garden — thymes, sages, lavender, a coffeeberry, and flannelbush. Heritage roses came mostly from a local rose nursery. There were many small niche nurseries on the coast of local gardeners, as well as commercial nurseries, including a succulent nursery that had over a hundred different varieties.

Unexpectedly, and a surprise to me, my garden was chosen as a selection for the annual garden tour in 2010, a June fund-raiser put on by the Mendocino Art Center. My half acre could not compete with the usual array of fine estate gardens kept manicured by in-residence landscapers. "Yours is real, more like what Fort Bragg represents," the committee chair said.

It had class, I assumed, as in "working-class," and it certainly involved a lot of work: the daily watering, weeding, and inspection to rout out snails, discern damage from voles and moles, or rampaging raccoons. I had to keep up with dead-heading roses, pruning rampant growth of shrubs and trees, checking the fruit trees for insect damage, dividing and replanting the irises. There was the annual trimming of fruit trees and topping of the Japanese maples as I climbed up a ladder with shears and saw. The wheelbarrow got good use, and so did my English garden spade.

The pond in the pot attracted tiny tree frogs in the spring, dragonflies laid their eggs in it, and a young hawk once perched on its rim for a few days of rest before flying off, but it was also a continual problem. Raccoons used it as their playpen, dislodging the fountain apparatus and tossing out the water lilies. I, in turn, had to unplug the pump, plunge my arm into cold water to reattach tubing, replant the lilies, reposition the pump. This litany could go on and on, but I truly enjoyed these chores, something people not attracted to mucking through dirt may not understand.

I also liked to repurpose debris or junk to fit into the garden. A leaking fifty-foot hose became edging for a dirt path along the tree-choked perimeter. A bathroom sink made a fine container for succulents. Rusty old tools decorated the side of the well house/potting shed. An iron headstand from an old bed frame, salvaged from an estate sale, served to keep roses confined to the garage wall. Some gardeners followed strict rules about spacing, soil mix, fertilizers, and grooming. For me it was more about becoming enamored by some plant, buying it, sticking it in whatever space I could find, and hoping it wouldn't die.

My father noticed my interest in gardens as I grew up. He told me he remembered only one thing from his childhood in a Sephardic community in Turkey: how to prune fig trees. Many years later, when my parents lived in L.A., he planted a fig in his backyard. It was all he wanted to take care of; the rest was yard work, he said, and he left that to the hired gardener. It was what he called yard work that most interested me. I planted a fig tree, too. Fort Bragg wasn't warm enough for figs to develop, but warm enough for me.

One day, digging out weeds, I uncovered an old brick path that led to the apple tree. If I needed a brick, I knew where to find one. The apple was a "King of Tompkins County," I surmised, after a visit to the annual Mendocino Apple Fair in Boonville. The apples were huge, prolific, and tasty, and their waxy skins deterred insect invasions. I added three more apple trees to join the pear, plum, and apricot trees. (Can one ever have too many apples? Yes, but then there are neighbors who are happy to have some.)

Five of seven evergreen oak seedlings I dug up from the yard of Kim's old apartment house grew into mature trees over the years, to add to the large maples and pine on the north side of the garage. The fog of summer days was captured by their leaves, and given the high-water table and sandy loam, conditions were perfect for tree roots. The daily watering I did each morning was for the more shallow-rooting shrubs, flowers, and berries. My time spent gardening was fully rewarded. Think of those apples and plums and berries bestowed on you in exchange for a little care, I told myself. Look at those colorful roses blooming their hearts out, and the irises—the ones saved just in time from the herds of snails.

A fellow turned up one day who had known the previous owners, and he solved the puzzle of buried asphalt paving. "The north side is low," he said, "so Art dumped asphalt and other stuff there to build it up. Art's garage used to be in the rear next to the fruit trees, and Mary's little sewing room used to be in front of the circular drive." It would have faced the street, where she could see neighbors walking by. "They brought trees from Missouri," the man said, "and planted blueberries in front of the redwoods"—the same area where I planted mine, as it turned out.

They probably planted the cottonwoods, too, one of which now towered over the redwoods along the back fence. It was a glorious tree that dropped thousands of golden leaves in the fall. It also provided a convenient landing for migrating birds, like hawks and flocks of cedar waxwings. Thanks to the mix of trees and shrubs and the bird-feeders we were constantly re-filling, and the pond that served as a birdbath, the garden became a way station for all kinds of birds throughout the year. A mockingbird liked to nest in the cottonwood until nearby resident ravens ravaged its eggs. The big window by the dining table in the kitchen, with its view out the back deck to the pond and garden, was perfect for bird-watching. I kept binoculars nearby, and a small notebook to record daily sightings.

Years back I had read a book titled *Earth Mazes* by Alex Champion. He wrote that "the labyrinth symbolizes the tortuous cyclic journey that each of us must take daily, . . . " Alex had devoted himself to building labyrinths across the world. I wanted one too, but it took me a long time to figure out how to do it. Partly this was because I didn't know I wanted one until I discovered how transporting the experience of following a labyrinth could be. The area where I had planted blueberries, bordered by redwoods and native plants, would be a good place for a labyrinth, I finally decided, except for all those blueberries.

Unconsciously, in the way fate works, things began to come together. I bought a couple of big concrete stepping-stones shaped like turtles. They could've gone anywhere, and therefore they went nowhere. They rested next to the tool shed for a month. Then a bull pine dying of bark beetle intrusions lost its last living limb. I called a tree guy who came out the next day and cut the pine into logs each about two feet high. Not having a fireplace, I wondered what I could do with those logs. Maybe, instead of digging a labyrinth into the ground, I could just mark it out with these logs.

I started walking in circles around the blueberries, and realized there was enough space for a three-circled snake labyrinth that could be bordered by upright logs. At the center were three blueberries. I placed one of the turtles there and the other at the entry point. I brought in a couple of other large stones to help set it off and found some daffodil bulbs to place around the perimeter. I felt very happy as I walked in circles, shaded and sheltered in that far corner by redwoods.

Control was a recurring message when I read about other people's gardens, and a real necessity for me. I was often out in that landscape I had made, like a figure in a drawing. I'd be bent over early in the morning to survey snail damage, catching a few in the act. I'd walk out to the compost pile after dinner and notice one of the ravens watching me from the garage roof, hoping for a handout. I'd be inspecting the pines for beetle damage, ready with my pruning saw to cut out a damaged limb. Once I noticed a butterfly struggling to escape a spider web and was able to release it. Other times I'd come upon a dead mouse or bird and knew a cat had come in the night. Once a doe showed up, having somehow squeezed past the side gate. Animal control arrived to encourage her to leave, and I added a fresh barrier to the gate.

On the day of the garden tour, we set up informational handouts at the picnic table under the apple tree. Kim and I often, during the summer and fall, played Scrabble there in the afternoons. Kim put together a display of before and after photographs, along with a photo album. We enjoyed telling people—more than 150 of them came through that day—how our garden had come to be. We encouraged the children to go exploring. This was a place where plants could be touched and paths were easy to follow; they wouldn't become lost, nor mess up anything. They could hide back there, the way I liked to do. I'd be that ghostly figure at twilight, weaving between the redwoods and maples, melting into the landscape, looking past flowers and pond at the deck with its climbing pink rose. I wanted to know and inhabit my true, still-alive self, that self I was as a young girl, who refused to match herself to how girls were supposed to behave and dress. I wanted to be, simply, me, in this garden I'd made, a place that offered a kind of tranquil companionship of uncritical being.

Perennial Life

Stephani Hemness

WE ESCAPED THE CITY to see the tulips in Skagit Valley, Washington, where crisp rows of color stripe a land backdropped by the Cascade mountains and a clear blue sky. In April, at least back then, there would still be visible snow in the mountains, adding more contrast to the already striking scene. We walked amongst the rows of flowers, still muddy from spring showers, and crouched near the blooms to take photos. We loved tulips, so vivid and upright after a wet and dreary winter. I snapped a photo of my mom standing in front of a row of deep purple tulips. Something about dark hued flowers and foliage appealed to her.

At her memorial service not even four years later, someone sent a basket of potted house plants, including some tulips. I took them in, glad to have something to nurture that would last longer than cut stems. But most of the plants died almost as suddenly as she did. The ones that are still alive today are the tulip bulbs I planted in the front of her house. They are a bright, spunky reddish orange. Not a deep hue that she would have chosen, but still pretty.

Spotting even a single tulip bloom sprouting from the soil sparks something like a surprise, a hope, a reminder; a short-lived beauty, but an intentionally planted bulb that returns year after year. Tulips have come a long way since they were first brought to Europe from the Ottoman Empire. Single, rare bulbs would decorate the gardens of the first privileged few. Now, we can buy thousands of different varieties of the perennial bulb and happily grow them in abundance. Like lilies, tulips come from true bulbs, inside which contain their stems and layered leaves, feeding from the soil through the winter. Near the red-orange tulips by the front window, I've since planted some white tulips as well, and each spring I hopefully await their return. Inheriting my mom's house gave me the opportunity to try my hand at gardening, and I've since learned that a garden is always changing, never truly a finished project. In the early days of missing my mom, planting and growing things gave purpose to my days. It was helpful to work with my hands, to do something tangible, tactical, and real in the moment. It's given me something to create and care for, year after year, during a difficult time that I've come to learn is never truly finished, either.

My mom was not really a gardener, but she loved flowers, and so do I. Even just growing some annuals in a pot on the front steps can be so satisfying. I took special care in the backyard too. It is quieter there, usually just me and the birds. No watching neighbors or housing association to dictate what can or cannot be done. No shame for the occasional dandelion. What began in the back with me planting a few dahlia tubers – in the deep blood red my mom would like – soon sparked a desire to plant and grow more in the space I was given, which at the time was only grass and overgrown weeds. I felt like Mary Lennox, given a chance to enliven a quiet space that would become my own.

With the help of my dad, I began by clearing out a large patch of grass to replace with perennials. The rest was up to me, and I relished the task of transforming the space. I had planned it so that each month a flower would greet me, starting in April with the white cherry tree, rooted there since the house was built twenty years ago. May would mark the three lilacs I had planted along the fence to freshen the bright spring air, usually in time for Mother's Day. I chose a purple and two white varieties, adopted from Hulda Klager Gardens. Because the backyard is southwest facing, I needed to plant what could also survive the heat and the sun of the summers. Thankfully, many perennial flowers love the sun, and so I planted them in the fall to ensure they had time to settle in before the following spring.

By the end of May, the thyme would bloom and buzz with bees. By June I'd enjoy the white sun roses with their yellow centers. July came the English lavender's soothing scent and more busy, well-fed bees. More pleasing purple would show up in the salvia, and the pale Bluebeard. August brings the beginning of the sedum blooms, first pale pink then deepening to mauve by September's end. The years I planted dahlias were the best in fall, a last hurrah of the long summer, easing into autumn with bold, spiky petals that competed with the changing leaves, which are often already brown and crunchy at the end of extra dry summers.

But I can no longer determine exactly when the seasons and the flowers will come, and how long they'll stay. The flowers bloomed early and left quickly last year, prompted by an unusually heated May. During a fifty-degree December last, my ranunculus bulbs started to come up, confused. Of course, plants respond to temperature and moisture and not to our calendars, which no longer align with the weather. We never expect to lose someone too soon, and we never expect many of the changes that a garden can also bring. I expected the normal progression of life, lilacs that bloom in time for a Mother's Day with my mom. I did not expect lilacs in April or spending most of my adult life without her.

Still, I keep growing things because I can. I try to practice patience with myself, and with the plants as we navigate the cycles, however wary. On the other side of the back garden, I began to focus on growing simple herbs like oregano, lemon thyme, lemon balm, and pineapple sage. More than the soft floral of roses or lilac, I love the citrus scent. Lemon lifts me up, travels up my nose and lands directly in my mind like a bright spark. I keep coming back, rubbing the leaves between my fingers and sniffing them to capture the feeling, however brief. As well as smelling good, I can use them practically for cooking, cocktails, and other concoctions. I enjoy the relative ease and consistency of growing perennial herbs, and I love them not just for their usefulness, but to simply sniff. To grow something to simply be, and to keep on being just for the sake of it.

Scent has the strongest ties to memory. And though these specific citrus scents don't remind me of her, my mom did have a strong sense of smell, and was sensitive to it. Perhaps that is why lilies were another of her favorite flowers, so fragrant and affecting. She had planted many white lilies in the front of her house to greet her as she arrived home each summer evening. Those lilies have since gone, but I've planted a few more in a pot in the front. Also true bulbs, lilies can spend the winter months feeding from the deep dark soil. The bulbs I planted have started to sprout already in a warm, early spring.

I don't know exactly which variety of lily bulbs my mom had first planted, but I like to think they looked like *Lilium Candidum*, sometimes called the Madonna Lily. Originally from the Mediterranean, it has been cultivated for thousands of years. The early Christians dedicated this variety to Mother Mary, and the white petals have come to symbolize purity and love. The lily also became a cultural symbol in France, known as the fleur-de-lys. My mom held an affinity to her French ancestry that manifested in a love of travel to Paris and for the symbol of the fleur-de-lys. Paris was the last place we ever visited together. The white lilies she planted returned for maybe another year or two after she died. Perhaps my mistake was not removing the bulbs from the soil to preserve them, assuming they would always return. But I suppose that is part of the learning process of growing things.

The ecology of my plot, this life of mine, is doing the best it can with what it has. There is less predictability now. Storms, droughts, sudden cardiac arrest. The arrhythmic climate is like the arrhythmic beat of my mother's heart. No longer being able to trust the weather, I still desire to grow something, to nurture life in any form. To stop to appreciate the fleeting sights, scents, and memories of it all. To live at all is such a miracle, I still marvel at its many forms. I still take joy in the fleeting spring and mourn the goings of winter, with hope still budding below the surface of the soil. I sniff the roses and remember her at Butchart Gardens. I watch a lily grow and bloom and remember her bright face. The tulips and lilies will eventually lose their petals, then leaves, then the remaining stems to be cut back. But the bulbs remain, still there on the other side of the soil. Intentionally planted, waiting patiently for next time. Perennial life.

Wish Fulfillment in a Garden

Cecile Mazzucco-Than

I WAS NEVER ONE for surprises in my life or in my gardens. My mother taught me to always keep the cookie jar filled, always arrive five minutes early, and never tell anyone my birthday. My father taught me to look under every leaf, enrich the soil, and plant in straight rows. My entire life I've been able to avoid tardy marks and surprise parties, hornworms and untidy beds. However, between tacitly acknowledging that I was at an over-the-hill age and embracing the challenge of an excavated front yard, I finally understood the secret to planting the garden of my dreams.

My father gardened from necessity. Constant hunger during the Great Depression taught him the importance of nurturing the body, and life after his service in World War II taught him the importance of nurturing the soul. My mother, also a member of the Greatest Generation, was a woman who stepped in to do one of the jobs servicemen left behind, and by the time the war ended, she was almost single-handedly running the local Five and Dime. More comfortable sizing up new salesclerks than nurturing seedlings, she gardened because her husband did.

They lived a post-war ideal — a quiet life in a gray Cape Cod my father and his brothers built themselves on a lot that his family had farmed. Located at the end of the city bus line, my father had room to garden, and my mother could be at work in fifteen minutes. Although he no longer needed to plant rows of savoy cabbages to stockpile for winter, my father still reserved the sunniest part of the backyard for an eating garden, with vegetables like zucchini and cucumbers perched on soft dirt mounds and tomatoes spaded deep into the soil. He circled the house with dahlias as big as a man's fist and never-ending waves of petunias. The same way my mother tabulated every nail and 2x4 to avoid housebuilding surprises, she streamlined my father's watering, weeding, and fertilizing to avoid blights, pests, and droughts, and yield a bounty they shared with the neighborhood.

By the time I toddled into the garden, we had moved to a new house with a white picket fence, towering oak trees in the front yard, and a pond to swim in at the edge of the backyard. I was so eager to shape moist earth for squash hills and bite into sun-warmed tomatoes, everyone assumed I'd been born with a green thumb, but at first, I gardened because my parents did. I helped my father turn the vegetable plot over in the spring and plant seedlings. If I spotted an unfortunate fish floating belly-up in the pond, I'd hold my nose and scoop it out. Burying a decaying fish into the tomato bed made me feel like I was living out the earth mother vibe that permeated the 1970s, as well as my grade school history books where Native Americans planted fish and corn together.

The former homeowner had been president of her garden club, so our flower beds were already rich with interesting plants. I soon had favorites – the orange and black speckled tiger lilies, petals curled back like a mane; the green and maroon striped Jacks-in-the-pulpit with an awning that hid the preacher, and the tall, fragrant, purple lilacs. I helped my mother add touches of her own, hybrid bearded irises chosen with care from catalogues, an unintentional tribute to the former owner, and zinnia and cosmos for flowers she remembered from her grandmother's garden from Woolworth's seed packets.

My father, who taught me to set out saucers of beer to prevent slugs from sampling the tomatoes and examine the underside of the plants' leaves for hornworms, interspersed basil, oregano, beans, and marigolds to avoid pests and welcome pollinators. My mother, who taught me to bake cookies in case anybody dropped in for a visit, put a 1960s-era cellophane hair bonnet in my pocket in case of rain and a bouquet of lilacs in my hand for my teacher. I anticipated the scent of lilies of the valley every spring, and every winter I avoided surprises and potential disappointments by scouring closets for Santa's presents.

My path to gardening and a well-planned existence had been so smooth I thought I'd coast into my own marriage with a life-long gardener. Instead, I fell in love with a man born on a desert island where fresh water was so expensive, backyard gardens were rarer than rain. I was so surprised by the Mondis, the forests of cacti taller than the few wizened Fofoti and Divi Divi trees bent over by the trade winds, we could have been honeymooning on the lunar surface. As beautiful as the island flora was, for me, Nature alone can plan and plant the desert.

That autumn we moved out of my parents' home and nearly 200 miles northeast to our own home that bordered a protected forest and a working farm. My widowed mother, my father's garden tools, and a few of the hybrid iris rhizomes from the flower beds came with us. We scratched the irises into the soil by the garage door, and I thought that would be the extent of our gardening. By spring, however, I needed to plant more than metaphorical roots. I just didn't know where. The foundation beds were dominated by mature, fuchsia azaleas, stubby pines with nesting robins that wouldn't let us open our front door, and verbena whose heavy perfume I invited into the house by cracking the windows at night.

I picked up my father's sturdiest shovel, the tip of its blade worn thin from decades of piercing the earth, and I started digging in a grass-less rectangle the former owners used for their daughter's swing set. My husband grabbed a hoe, collaring and breaking hunks of dirt and raking the patch smooth. Once tomatoes and peppers marched in straight rows, and several hills of zucchini nestled in the corners, my husband suggested adding eggplants and sunflowers. I nicknamed him Jans Boer, John-the-farmer, in his second native language. Unlike the Divi Divi that cannot flourish anywhere but its desert island, my husband came into his own gardening in the deciduous forest of the Eastern seaboard.

When I proposed replacing the slab of grass in the back with a bower and a wisteria arbor arching over a cement bench, my husband took me to the two-for-one sale at the nursery featured on *This Old House*. We bought two tree-form hydrangeas and planted them a good doorway width apart to form a fragrant entrance. Some months later, we called that same nursery to remove a mountainous Purple Gem rhododendron from the curb where the snowplow turned it into Frosty the Snowman every winter and transplant it to anchor the bower just to our left as we stepped between the hydrangeas. Hunks of the shrub crumbled off as the crew dragged it across the lawn on its burlap magic carpet, and my husband and I transplanted those densely rooted pieces around the perimeter of the property, alternating them with slips of forsythia that we culled from a larger plant growing wild in the side yard.

My mother suggested a hosta garden under the pine tree that towered over the north side of the house after a neighbor offered us a few pips as she separated the hostas by her mailbox. One by one, we chose from nurseries and catalogue-varieties to complement that gift: plants with narrow, golden-green leaves to balance those with wide, white-edged leaves, varieties with bluish green leaves for accents. The circlet under the tree filled into a full moon. We could almost tell how old the garden was by counting the rings of hostas.

We planned every planting and molded serendipity as if we were pseudo – Frank Lloyd Wright fitting the landscape around our well-structured dream house, orchestrating surprises via well-thought-out pops of color. My first pregnancy, also a product of careful planning, temperature taking, and counting calendar days, was hard won against my less-than-optimal age. I left no room for surprises as I watched my diet, exercised, limited my travel. I insisted on my final ultrasound just two days before my due date, so I'd know the sex of my child before the obstetrician announced it. My husband's suggestion for a lily garden to replace the mulched figure eight that the previous owners had snaked between two tall pines close to the front door was calculated to be therapeutic. All the squatting and gentle pulling and bearing down to weed that continued into the final weeks of pregnancy, my biological clock ticking in unison with the rhythm of the seasons, eased my mind more completely than Lamaze class and guided my daughter into perfect position for entering the world.

The Casablanca lily's huge, luminescent white flowers became a favorite background for photos of our toddler. Friends who received these snapshots nicknamed her "The Lily" because she toiled not and neither did she spin, but she was as beautiful in her baby-ness as the flower in its glory. The fall she turned one, we sat her on top of a pumpkin we had grown. My friend had sent her a cable-knit sweater with a farm tractor stitched into a patch on the front, as much a tribute to the quasi-farming area we lived in as a wish that my child would grow into the next generation of gardeners.

The Casablanca's spicy perfume wafting through the early morning or evening air inspired us to start a scent garden on the sunny side of the house. The wisteria arbor, in spite of its rickety construction and paucity of blooms, would be the focal point. I remembered many happy hours as a teenager spent lounging on the backyard chaise smelling the lilacs on warm afternoons, and I wanted my children to experience the same. My mother remembered some of the varieties we had, and we bought and planted lilacs until a stagger of starter shrubs stumbled away from the hulking rhododendron and followed the line of our neighbor's combination stone wall and chain-link fence. However, by the time a lone spray of blooms unfolded on one of Miss Kim's slender branches, we were set to move again, this time to Long Island.

Three tree-form PeeGee hydrangeas in the side lot of our new home eased the pain of leaving our unfinished gardens behind. Our family had grown to two toddlers, the second as carefully planned as the first. They soon followed that side lot into the back and started building fairy houses between the gnarly toes of the trees. Delighted, we talked about setting stepping-stones to ramble into the gloom and twist around soon-to-be-planted hostas, Jacks-in-the-pulpit, astilbes, lilies of the valley, broken-clay-pot toad houses, and odd garden statuary that would tempt all the sprites my girls could imagine to their fairy Levittown.

An inground pool occupied the ideal spot for growing vegetables, so my mother proposed a container garden on the patio. My husband and I filled a dozen planters from wine-cask to 100-cup-coffee-urn size with sweet, enriched loam, and propped a trellis at the back of several. In the chill of early April, my mother filled one chubby palm from each of my toddlers with pea seeds and let the girls drop the seeds in a shallow trench in front of each trellis then cover them with dirt. By the time the peas flowered and formed, I guided my daughters in using a trowel to bite deep into the earth and pull back enough to slip in a tomato seedling as if they were tucking it under the covers. Later, we filled more pots with petunias, portulaca, snapdragons, marigolds, and at least two small hibiscus, called *Kayena* in my husband's first native language, as a tribute to the beauties of his birthplace.

My daughters gardened because we did, but they didn't take to it from the moment they poked a pea seed into the soil. They watered and weeded a little to share time with us, but they preferred dancing around the inground sprinklers in their bathing suits to digging in the dirt. As much as they enjoyed looking at and smelling the flowers, just glimpsing a sun-ripened cherry tomato didn't make their mouths water and their heads spin with plans for expanding the patio garden. We never could coax them to taste even one of the first early peas, never mind a handful just seconds out of the shell.

Before the girls were ready to give up running under the sprinklers on the front lawn they were forced to by the unexpected. Despite several years of careful use, our family of five overburdened our home's aging cesspool, and my husband and I decided to replace it before the situation turned into a crisis. We didn't realize that replacing it would mean digging up the entire front yard. For all our gardening experience, we never anticipated that beneath the skin of grass there was no topsoil or even a thick layer of dirt, just a bottomless layer of sand – the best cement-making sand on Long Island, the cesspool contractor told us. He assured us that if we could dig out enough of it, say enough to replace it with a diving-depth swimming pool to match the one in the back, he could sell it for top dollar.

Our lot, perched on an enormous prehistoric sand dune, was a microcosm of the macrocosm of the island itself, soil with an excellent percolation rate, but impossible for residents like my husband and I, and our collection of shovels from my father's garage, to turn into a lawn and garden, lush or sparse, without help. After surveying enough dredged up pseudo-beach to turn the front yard into our own version of a desert island, or what the girls called Roo's Sandy Pit, we did something we'd done many times in our gardening lives and something we'd never done: We sat on the front steps with a cup of coffee and dreamed of how we wanted the yard to look, and then we called in a landscaper.

The excavated yard in front of us was the proverbial blank canvas. We didn't have to work around the previous owner's plantings even if they might have been garden-club quality. We could plan every sapling, seedling, or rhizome of our choice before a neighbor derailed our plans with a surprise clump of daylilies or hostas. I felt like my father must have felt once their dream house was built, and he surveyed the churned-up yard designating places for the vegetables and the flowers. I could have lilacs and a wisteria trellis. My mother could have beds with four o'clocks and hollyhocks. We'd leave a barely respectable, handkerchief-sized lawn. We even made a few sketches on the backs of the day's mail.

Our landscaper, a native Long Islander, listened to all our wishes and suggested a few touches of his own: a brick path with plenty of swoop, swoosh, and drama to transport visitors to the front door, and a blanket of sod to immediately warm the front yard with lush pile. Then, he offered, "Why don't you let me do everything for you?" He would make all our dreams a reality at the same time, so maybe just this once, we would be able to finish a garden and enjoy it before we had to move.

For a split second, as I surveyed the sand farm our cesspool replacement left behind, I felt like I had won the once-in-a-lifetime gardening lottery. I welcomed the landscaper's offer of the striking brick walkway and suggested a herringbone pattern. Our attempt at laying a running brick path to the front door of the house we sold resulted in a rutted road any ancient Roman would scorn. I embraced his offer of a plush sod lawn instead of seed because instant grass was like waving a magic wand, and I accepted his offer to shape the planting beds to snuggle the perimeter and wait under the trees because, even without fiftieth birthday surprise parties, my husband and I were beginning to feel the limits of our physical strength. However, I refused his offer to fill those planting beds even though he promised to put in every flower or shrub I had ever wished for.

I imagined filling those beds with treasures from future years of field trips to botanical gardens, arboretums, nurseries, and PTA plant sales. We had already found a place in the patio pots for the Dixie-cup-grown pole beans my daughters brought home from kindergarten. But most of all, looking at those beds made me remember that gardeners are not born but made, and always need room to grow.

For my daughters, branching out from fairy gardens to butterfly or pollinator or eating gardens would be like making up their minds to try one bite of a freshly picked tomato. From a first bite, or sometimes after a second or third, they might develop a taste that lasts a lifetime. I decided I would lightly and gradually populate the front yard beds because I am rarely happier than when I'm digging plants into the earth, but I would make sure to leave plenty of room there in case my daughters decided to join me, or my neighbors decided to surprise me with gifts of thinned out hostas, daylilies, or peonies.

In a garden, I concluded, serendipity is wish fulfillment, and planting — the sweetest, most cherished part of gardening and garden dreams — depends on serendipity. For all my devotion to avoiding surprises by careful planning in my life and in my gardens, the best and most meaningful gardens evolved slowly from my own hands and the hands of those I loved working the soil one plant at a time, acquired by calculation or by chance, and the gardens I remembered most fondly were never completed.

A Symphony of Nature: Rewilding My Garden in the Alps

Michaela Emch

IN THE HEART OF *the majestic Alps, where snow-capped peaks meet verdant valleys, a symphony of nature unfolds in the form of a rewilded garden. This haven, basking in the southern sun, is not just a patch of greenery but a thriving ecosystem that pulsates with life. Nestled in this serene landscape is a rejuvenated pond, the focal point of a mesmerizing dance of biodiversity that has flourished in a remarkably short span.*

I can hear the rain droplets hitting the surface of the pond. I can hear the liquid noises the sparrows' feet make on the copper gutter as they evaluate if it is worth leaving their shelter to aim at the proverbial early worm. It is raining, it is springtime, and I love hearing all the different sounds of the soft awakening of nature after a harsh winter. It is like a new morning has broken after a long and unforgiving night.

The wonders of the circulation of energy among the soil, the plants, the birds, and small mammals that inhabit the direct surroundings of our chalet call life back into previously sleepy dead leaves, bare sticks, and cold mortarless stone walls. What seemed dead comes back to life.

I am glad to see that after only a few seasons of leaving nature alone, equilibrium is coming back to this small, sensitive, harsh, and formerly degraded ecosystem: the garden I have the privilege to be the custodian of. Humans call it ownership. I, for myself, definitely do not own all of the inhabitants of this little patch of land, bordering on the mixed forest overlooking the Rhone Valley in the Swiss Alps. Maybe, the garden owns me?

The sun is rising, as always at the Eastern tip of the valley, and it shines its first timid rays on the frosty soil, the dry grass, and decomposing leaves scattered on the bent down grass. Its magic touch awakens drops of water that were captured in the form of ice beneath the sharp stones holding up the arches under which I store firewood. The gentle solar glow and energy revives some dwellers of the spruce and the larch's root system. As the rays become more vertical, the energy flow is now picking up. Water starts to circulate, balsamy warmth beams energy to seeds, roots, and hibernating limbs of insects and frogs. It raises the temperature of soil and air, allowing for interactions that had been set on hold for a few months. Starting a still lazy conversation: "It has been a long time since we have touched, are you still my symbiotic partner?" The awakening is slow, timid, cautious.

Within a few days, all processes of communication are back in full swing. The various tits are exploring crevices in trees and under my roof to prepare their nests. Frogs and toads move in slow processions to the pond in search for a mate after a long, solitary winter hiding in shelters between earth and roots. The slightly warming nights are filled with their serenades to attract potential partners – adding a typical spring sound to the previously almost silent evenings. The sleepy insects rub their ankylosed limbs and stretch their wings, moving their antennae, capturing scents and cues. They are looking for the best place to lay their eggs.

Happiness fills my heart as I can now, after a couple of years of helping the local ecosystem to restore its ancient ways, enjoy the presence of dozens of species of Alpine birds, their melodies fill the air, some trills, some shrieks, some elaborate songs, some very discreet murmurs. I spend a few minutes every morning listening with my eyes closed to identify the authors of these messages, their locations and their numbers. A quiet and reconnecting meditation. The chitter-chatter accompanies my morning cup of tea on the balcony as I watch in awe the sunrise and the Alpenglow painting the rocky, snowy, and icy slopes with every morphing hue of pink and orange. The clouds are the master painters of the sky and delight me with abstract masterpieces every morning. Adding depth and life to the ether.

Soon it will be time for the swallows to return from their African journey and plaster my roof's corner with their muddy sculptures holding their peeping babies – ever hungry and demanding for their parents' attention. Butterflies will unfold their wings, crickets will start stridulating, hedgehogs and weasels will hunt their prey at crepuscule and play their essential part in the equilibrium of natural processes. Lizards will warm their bodies on the stones heated by the sun, ready to catch the tiny flying bugs they favor for their lunch. A few weeks later, when days get longer, all the deciduous trees will have unrolled their leaves to make the most of the sun's rays, transforming pure light into matter while also providing shade to the squirrels running up and down their trunks and spying on their colleagues raising their babies in cushioned nests.

As the season progresses, hovering gracefully above the pond, dragonflies emerge as guardians of the garden. Beyond their aesthetic appeal, these creatures play a pivotal role in maintaining ecological harmony by preying on mosquitoes and other pests. Their presence is not just functional; it adds a poetic layer to the rewilded space, symbolizing the delicate balance achieved through nature's intricate choreography. Following the completion of their lifecycle into their imago form, they are now obsessed with sending their genes into the future through reproduction. And this is where the pond, again, plays a central role. Providing drinking water is one of its functions, but providing a site where to place your eggs or larvae is an even more crucial role this small body of water plays in the ecosystem. Especially as it is the only stagnant water miles around in this dry prairie environment. This makes it a magnet for all biodiversity: insects, amphibians, and mammals converge, each at their designated time, to make the most of this modest waterhole.

The resident badgers like water too, but what they really love is to dig up the carrots and lettuce I planted in the spring. They emerge from their burrows, embarking on forays that contribute to the health of the soil through their digging and foraging activities. Maybe my modest vegetable offerings are the price to pay for such a lovely multispecies neighborhood?

Even a very discreet visitor likes to contemplate its reflection under the rising moon. Welcome to my resident slithering companion, the viper that calls the compost heap its home. As it lurks in the rotting vegetation, it embodies the feeling of quiet impermanence we feel when we watch nature up close. When at first glance everything seems quiet and constant in the garden, the feeling of peace evanesces as soon as we observe the subtle processes at play. Predators ambushing their prey. The beauty of spiderwebs is the manifestation of a deadly trap. The silent flight of the owl at night signifies an almost certain death for a few rodents who will not see the light of the next dawn. While this may seem cruel to us humans, nature has no morals, no intentions, good or bad – and this is just the way balance is maintained or restored to favor the perpetuation of life at the level of the community of all living things. A permanent imbalance looking for balance in the long run! Maybe there is something for us to learn from the continuous fluctuations in energy, resources, roles, and environment that allows us to achieve overall acceptance and equilibrium.

Nature knows. Are we ready to listen? And to watch? And to sense?

My skin is now already reacting to a new morning freshness as the seasonal cycle moves on. The light is turning yellow, leaves start to change color, ever so slightly. No doubt, fall is on the horizon. If I am careful, I can notice the change in behavior of my furry and winged friends: squirrels gather nuts and roots, swallows gather in the trees, getting ready for their long voyage to the South, the coat on the fallow deer I catch a glimpse of every now and then grows thicker. And here he is, for the first time this season, the majestic deer, passing behind the tree line, as silent as a ghost, moving down from his summer pastures, getting to lower altitudes where food is available as the first frost bites his higher territory. The gentle presence and elegant gaze of the females composing his herd become integral components of the winter tableau, adding a touch of grace to the rewilded haven.

In the undergrowth, the unnoticed heroes of the rewilded garden get ready for the slow season. These are small mammals that often escape the human eye. From industrious shrews to elusive voles, these creatures contribute to the interconnected web of life within our haven. In me they foster a sense of stewardship for this garden, and they help me appreciate the intricate dance of life unfolding in my own backyard.

I am proud of my rewilding efforts, even though nature did most of the heavy lifting: restoring broken processes, filling each bare patch of soil with life, restoring impermanent balance, calling in species that had been pushed away by too much human interference. It is a wonder to watch how this rich tapestry of life is adaptable, beautiful, and resilient.

I would like to encourage every one of us to rewild our gardens. And maybe rewilding extends far beyond our individual gardens. Let us join a collective movement towards a more harmonious relationship with nature. Let us reach out to our communities about the benefits of rewilding, let us organize gatherings, workshops, and share success stories. The magic of the result, a beautiful, wild, interesting, fascinating object of reflection, awe and discovery is all we need to reconnect to ourselves, our surroundings, our rhythms, and all the inhabitants of the spaces we are the stewards of.

Let us enjoy a rewilded garden and – maybe cultivate a rewilded secret garden in our minds, connecting to our ancestral relationship to all living things – for a more balanced, (bio)diverse and respectful future.

My Gardens, My Children. My Children, My Gardens.

Carolyn Doepke Bennett

"I THINK YOU LOVE your garden more than you love me!"

That was my frustrated seven-year-old trying to draw my attention away from deadheading my midsummer blooms so that I could admire her mastery of hula-hooping on the driveway. She was right, there *were* moments when I loved my garden more than her! My garden didn't talk back to me, refuse to eat what I fed it, or need a "time out" for bad behavior.

I have three children, but my garden was another living thing that I cared for. And it cared for me. It nourished my soul, provided calm in the midst of chaos, and satisfied my need for aloneness. Like my children, it presented its share of heartbreaks, challenges, and growing pains – broken limbs, surprising diseases, stubborn behaviors. But also like my children it could bring me to tears of gratitude with sudden expressions of unselfish love in the form of glorious blossoms, succulent fruits, and just-off-the-vine vegetables.

But how to explain this deep-rooted love for a garden to my attention-demanding daughter, or to anyone, for that matter? I was about her age when it all started. It was summer. I was bored. My mother, distracted from what she was doing by my constant whining, reacted by frisbeeing me a leftover tin from last night's cherry pie and told me to go play outside. Obediently I took the plate and wandered into the woods enveloping our northern Michigan cottage.

I was immediately mesmerized by the domes of brilliant green moss dotting the forest floor among the gloomy rotting logs and crunchy dried leaves. I crouched down to examine them more closely and was surprised by their velvety touch and intricate patterning of teeny leaflets. They were virtually rootless. I easily lifted up several soft mounds and wedged them into the pie plate alongside some lacey ferns and needle-leafed baby evergreens. I added twigs and birch bark for decoration and proudly brought it back to show my mother. She loved it. That's all the approval I needed.

I mothered that moss pie garden the rest of the summer with sunshine and water and an occasional swap out for a dying fern. I lovingly held it on my lap during the nine-hour drive back to our suburban home in August. There it basked on a windowsill in my bedroom until winter came, and with it my moss pie garden's death . . . a death that hit me harder than the passing of my dime store turtle, Ulysses S. Grant, or our canary, Happy. The loss triggered my lifelong vow to make more gardens and keep my hands dirty.

That was over sixty years ago. Since then I've added many gardens to my homes and neighborhoods, from a rooftop garden above my fourth floor Chicago walk-up to a native plant garden in a drought stricken climate. Also a children's garden in a tarmacked school yard. A vegetable garden in a home for foster children. Each was as singular to me as my children.

My gardens and my children: unique and yet so alike in what they meant to me and what they gave to me. Both offered moments of amazement, days of joy, months of change, and years of learning. Of course they were also infuriating, frustrating, and temperamental! Were the gardens like my children or my children like my gardens?

They were all conceived with love and nourished in anticipation of what they would grow to become. And become they did. Sometimes much too fast for me. I couldn't slow them down despite my best motherly efforts. Like the Agave attenuata that shot its trunk-like asparagus bloom into the sky so fast I could see it grow daily in front of me. And the equally shocking moment when I 'suddenly' had to reach up to hug my son instead of reaching down to hold his hand.

Nourishment came in many forms. For my kids it was healthy breakfasts, daily homemade school lunches, and never-frozen dinners. For my plants I overcame my abhorrence of slimy things and started worm composting so that their soil would be enriched with fungus, bacteria, and essential nutrients. But even the best intentions fall flat. One spring an army of ants rallied the troops and invaded my outdoor composter, efficiently annihilating the unsuspecting worms. I spent months rebuilding their population and moved the plastic bin to the garage for protection only to have the entire worm colony fry in the summer heat.

My children were not immune from my intentions either. I chose one of my children's birthdays to make a delicious and healthy chocolate zucchini cake. The mistake wasn't making it with zucchini, it was telling them what was in it! You would have thought I'd said it was chocolate worm cake.

Gardens and children both occasionally need supporting, corralling, or cajoling which I provided with arches, trellises and lots of twine for the plants and playpens, treats and trips to Disneyland for the kids. My children managed to keep from strangling themselves in an old borrowed portable playpen now banned for its hazardous wooden slats. Treats were limited to food you couldn't buy at a gas station and Disneyland, only an hour away, was free because my husband worked for Disney at the time.

Although my climbing roses didn't need playpens, they did need supports, which I confess to acquiring under unusual, though legal (I think) circumstances. I had bought a lovely bare root heirloom rose. Dubbed the Rose of the Year in the UK, it was described as a double-flowered floriferous scented rambler in shades of blush to light apricot to honey champagne. It sounded delicious but in need of some training. I asked my London gardener to help make a support for them. He brought over some willow canes he had nicked from one of his clients' gardens and tied them into an arc with garden twine. "Won't they miss the willow?" I asked. "Not a problem," he said. "They are from Paul and Linda's." "McCartney?" I asked. "Yep. The very same." I let it slide as I didn't think the McCartneys would press charges and because the name of the rose was Penny Lane.

All of these devices were just methods of control for the good of both my human and plant families. It was hard not to believe I was in control. I was the adult in the room. For the most part it worked with my kids because I was bigger and louder than them and had the keys to the car. Not so in the garden where another mother was in charge: Mother Nature. I learned this the hard way. I once designed a lovely formal parterre garden around the focal point of a divine gnarly old apricot tree only to have the tree fall over dead the day after the garden was completed. Despite homemade concoctions and, I confess, some sprays with XXX's on the labels, slimy snails would always find my hostas, squirrels would eat every unripe persimmon overnight, and aphids from miles away must have bought first class seats to be the first to populate my early spring shoots.

I planted an English garden in California and then a California garden in England. Neither worked. The plants I attempted to grow in California inspired by my British gardening books either keeled over from the heat or instantly adapted and took over the warm and sunny beds. And when I planted a vegetable garden in the back of my nineteenth century London house, the only root vegetables I reaped were pieces of clay pipes, broken roof tiles, and shards of old blue and white pottery. I was told, too late, backyards in England were traditionally used for household refuse.

I learned from these mistakes. Through trial and error, I found that children, like plants, have minds of their own. I had to let my children thrive in their own world. As much as I wanted it to happen, my eight-year-old gymnast on the local YMCA team was not going to make it to the Olympics. Just because my younger daughter sang in a regional production of *Joseph and the Amazing Technicolor Dreamcoat* . . . it didn't mean one day she'd be thanking me while accepting a Tony Award. My role in the garden and in the house was letting my children bloom without getting in their way. That, and cutting oranges for soccer games.

Sooner than I expected, it was harvest time. I had done my work – planted, nourished, protected. The time had come to stand back and witness the results . . . relish my full blooming. Time to take a breath and cherish every quiet moment in my gardens and every noisy moment as a mom.

Gardens are not stagnant. Neither are children. Most of my gardens have morphed, changed with new ownership, faded away in all but my memory. My children, too, have changed but remain constant. I will never know what my gardens think of me, but I'm happy to see that some of my love of nature has rubbed off on my now-adult children, as they are all budding gardeners. They are strong enough to tote fifty-pound bags of manure, young enough to learn the Latin names of plants instead of the Home Depot ones, and impatient enough to make as many mistakes as I did. Spending the time I did, gardening was not one of my mistakes. It was a blessing. It made me a better mother. I think my children would agree if only because, when I was being embraced by my plants, they were free to be themselves.

I look down now at my vein-mapped hands frantically digging in the dirt of my herb garden trying to tear out the mint that has gone rogue. I knew better. I really knew better. You never plant mint if you don't want it to take over. But during the last few months of neglect due to my husband's ill health, it has done just that. Now, having received news that his disease has spread, I have done what I always do . . . gone into my garden for consolation and solace.

But I can't find it. I am so angry at the mint. I want to rip it out the way I want to rip his illness out. My bare fingers dig deep into the soil to find its hidden roots and extricate them without leaving bits behind. Get it all! That's the goal. I silently gloat when I can hold onto one tentacle long enough to watch it unwillingly come to the surface with all its hairy roots intact.

The mint is only doing what comes naturally, sending out its shoots of growth, spreading its wings. So much like my children. Why would I ever want to hold them back? They have been comforting me in ways my plants cannot. But my garden is comforting me now in its own ever-present way.

By the end of that recent day, only half the bed has been cleared. But that's OK. The other half is a rumpled mass of bright green mint whispering of health in the language we both understand. Lifting me out of my cloud of darkness. Slowly and calmly I uncreak my back, gently pinch off a few sprigs, and head inside. I put them in water on the kitchen windowsill and wash the healing dirt from my hands.

A Reluctant Gardener: Lessons on Nature From My Dogs

Sassafras Patterdale

I HAVE NEVER BEEN what someone might describe as outdoorsy. Outside was where I was to get from one place to another, not a place I looked forward to spending time. For most of my twenties the only ground I got into was the staircase descent into the New York subway system. Growing up my grandparents had an elaborate garden, and my relatives were actual farmers, but I never aspired to spend time growing anything. I preferred to spend my time in climate-controlled buildings only occasionally purchasing flowers from the corner bodega to brighten my small apartment homes. I grew up on the edges of suburbia and as a queer kid, I learned very quickly that being in nature wasn't always especially safe. I saw the way that LGBTQ+ people were targeted and excluded. I was told clearly that my queerness was not welcome. Like many other LGBTQ+ people after coming out, I naturally gravitated to the city. Today I'm writing from the hammock in my backyard. The smell of freshly cut grass. The wind is rustling in the trees above my head, my hands are dirty and stained from planting vegetables in my summer garden and there are pansies, canonical queer flowers blooming next to my front door.

In September 2012, I adopted Charlotte, a cattle dog shepherd cross who had been a street dog in South Carolina and was transported to NYC in hopes that she would find an adoptive home. I fell in love with Charlotte immediately. It was a magnetic attraction I've never experienced before or since. When I saw her with the rescue organization, I knew that she was meant to be my dog. Despite how impractical it was to bring home a second dog, I did. My other dog, Mercury was a small chihuahua who loved living in my Brooklyn apartment. He was more than satisfied with going outside quickly for bathroom breaks and then hurrying back inside. Charlotte, however, took great pleasure in the outside world and any opportunity she had to explore it. I began taking long daily walks with her through Prospect Park, aptly called the backyard of Brooklyn. Prospect Park became ours. I spent as much time as I could, no matter the weather: from steamy humid summers, watching her bury her face and plow through piles of autumn leaves, to the depths of fringed New York winters, where she raced through snow drifts while I ran alongside her. We spent hours following the scent trails of the urban wildlife through the park and I began to experience nature through Charlotte, seeing the magic and wonder of the natural world that just months before I hadn't paid any attention to.

A couple of years after I adopted Charlotte the management of my apartment changed. The apartment building went from a very traditional "if you aren't bothering anyone nobody is going to bother you" style New York apartment, to one filled with rules about what life in the building with dogs would be like. The new rules made it feel impossible to continue living there and give my dogs any quality of life. By this point, I had made it my priority to get Charlotte out into nature as much as possible, whenever and wherever I could. As a result, my partner at the time and I decided to move out of the trendy, fun, and close-in areas of Brooklyn to get a house at the end of the subway line to give Charlotte a better life.

I'll never forget the frigid December morning when Charlotte saw "her" yard for the first time. Charlotte had overcome a lot in her life, having survived on the streets where she raised a litter of puppies. I wanted to do anything in my power to give her a new life. As a dog trainer, intellectually, I know that dogs have a limited vocabulary. On a spiritual level, it was clear to me that Charlotte understood the house was hers. Her face lit up as she wandered room to room. Then, she tumbled out the door, leapt into her new backyard racing circles and chased a ball. I was so proud that I had been able to give her this.

Moving into the house I suddenly found myself responsible for a yard, "Charlotte's Yard," as I called it. Gardening wasn't really my thing, but for Charlotte it needed to be. The small yard was mostly mud and weeds when we moved in. It became one of my goals to make the yard into a place where we all wanted to spend time. I hoped that I could turn it into something nicer for her; I just had to figure out how. I started researching gardening online. I looked up dog-safe plants. Ultimately, I planted grass seeds and clover to create a green and lush area for her to play. My ex and I built raised flower beds and I planted flowers and tomatoes. Charlotte loved the opportunity to sit with me outside watching as the bees flew in and out of the towering sunflowers. Charlotte sniffed the baby plants poking through the dirt. She laid in the sun on the cracked cement patio, as I mowed the tiny lawn, taking in her surroundings and took pleasure in showing her giant breed "little" sister puppy around the yard when I brought her home a few months after we moved into the house. The yard became one of our favorite places, with the dogs enjoying the fresh air and escape from the concrete of life in New York City.

Two years later we moved cross-country, and my top priority was finding a bigger yard for Charlotte and the other dogs. Even the real estate brokers knew that the most important thing was finding the right house for my pack of high-needs dogs: no stairs for Sirius the Newfoundland who'd had major knee surgery, and a big backyard for the dogs to play, especially for Charlotte. I ruled out house after house because the yards were concrete, or smaller than what we had in New York. Eventually we found the perfect house, with a double lot, lots of grass, and fruit trees to provide shade. The real estate agent knew it was the right house for the dogs the minute they showed it to me, and the day we closed on the home they gifted the dogs new toys to enjoy in their backyard. Charlotte was aging quickly at this point, but when she saw her big yard, she raced like a puppy through the grass. Although I started gardening for Charlotte, I have continued to learn that I enjoyed the ritual of caring for plants. Mowing the lawn became my favorite household chore, and I started to look forward to visiting the garden center, selecting seeds to plant and watching them flourish. I'm not an exceptionally skilled gardener, but I have fun with it.

Over the years, the yard I have has changed. I traded postage stamp Brooklyn for double lot Portland. Over those years Charlotte passed, my ex-partner left, and now it's just me and "Charlotte's puppy" Sirius, the giant dog I brought home the winter after Charlotte got her first yard, now a senior dog herself. We spend as much time as we can in the yard. Today, Sirius lay dozing in the sun on my porch next to the pots of pansies as I planted tomatoes, zucchini, marigolds, and petunias into barrels. I still wouldn't consider myself particularly outdoorsy but for the dogs, I've learned how to explore the natural world. Charlotte taught me to start to enjoy nature on my own terms. Spending more time outside and spending time growing things for the dogs helps me to be calmer and more relaxed as a writer. I turned forty this year, and there is a special newfound joy in the simplicity of the life I share with my dog. I invite our queer chosen family to grill veggie burgers in the backyard with the flowers I planted blooming like our new life.

Charlotte overcame a lot in her life from a challenging beginning as well as a lot of health issues but she was also the most joyful dog I ever met. She loved exploring and playing and she inspired me to do the same. Charlotte has passed for many years now, and there isn't a day that goes by that I don't miss her or remember the lessons that she taught me. I especially enjoy the spring—planting flowers, watching seeds pop up, and seeing how much Sirius enjoys rolling and playing in the grass. I spend as much time as I can writing in my backyard in the hammock. Next to me, there is a concrete statue that looks like Charlotte, and one that resembles my tiny Mercury who despite having been a happy apartment dog also grew to enjoy exploring outside. I make sure there are always fresh flowers planted, the petunias stretching up around the concrete statues. Without Charlotte I don't think I ever would have understood the joys of being in nature. This is one of the many legacies that she has left me.

Ghost Garden

Connie Levesque

I sleep where the lilacs once grew, where honeysuckle crimped the wooden lattice outside the kitchen window. The scent of these ghost plants sometimes seeps into my dreams and I wake disoriented, the old house and garden so present to me still.

Ten years ago, we had our two-story house in Portland deconstructed and raised a single-story house in its place, a house we could age into surrounded by a garden I could truly call my own. Yet, no garden is truly one's own. It's a place ever evolving, subject to the vagaries of style, the whims of weather, to neighbors and aching backs and happenstance.

What befell my garden that rainy March was more an assault than an evolution. I'd heard the horror stories about home building, the stress on a marriage, the unexpected costs, but I wasn't prepared to see the garden, my little piece of Eden, reduced, if temporarily, to a kind of Hell. Though the project was of our own making, it was bittersweet watching our house dismantled, the roof stripped away, the floors and windows and fixtures hauled off to be repurposed, until the house that had held so many memories vanished, its surrounding garden forever altered.

The house was a rental when we moved to the narrow dead-end street, formerly called Orchard Lane, over forty years ago. It was situated on four-tenths of an acre surrounded by hedges, and rivaled an arboretum in its variety of trees. Spruce, birch, pine, cedar, maple, fir, persimmon, sweet-gum, oak, and mountain ash graced the lot, along with aged apple and pear trees, the latter, "gnarled widows of an orchard," the inspiration for my first published poem.

From the start, our house reminded me of my great-aunt's home in Seattle. Hers, too, was a modest white house with a garden shady enough for rhododendrons and sword fern. The flower beds at our rental felt familiar as well, with many of the plants that had graced my childhood home: Jupiter's beard, iris, daylily, forsythia, lilac, and honeysuckle.

That garden, on a corner lot in Tacoma, had been my sanctuary. I was the sixth of eight kids in a house that my mom had dubbed the big red barn. The house sometimes felt more like a zoo than a barn and I took refuge in the garden. I can still describe every flower and tree and edging stone of that garden. It was the blueprint for what a garden should be—bountiful, but wild, a little rough around the edges.

The garden at our Portland rental was certainly rough around the edges when we moved in. A neighbor casually mentioned how lovely the garden had looked under the former tenants. Not one to shy from competition, the pressure was on to prune the suckered fruit trees, tame the hedges, and weed the flower beds, to prove we were worthy garden successors.

I reveled in learning each new plant as it bloomed that first spring—grape hyacinth, leopard's bane, and leathery-leafed bergenia, but there were some villainous intruders as well. Buttercups morphed from yellow blooms to seeds that hitchhiked on gloves and pant legs. And I spent countless hours battling creeping Jenny, an invasive groundcover on a par with English ivy. But my true nemesis was the bluebell. The blossoms made for a lovely spring display, but the bluebells taunted me then, as they taunt me still, sprouting in our pathways, lurking under ferns and azaleas, horning in on a tidy patch of primroses.

It wasn't until we purchased the rental house that I could begin to shape our garden to my liking. Out came the holly tree by the front door; in went a path from the gravel drive. Out went the mountain ash with its squishy orange berries; in went a Japanese maple and gingko, generously gifted for our wedding. But Mother Nature insisted on lending a hand with the garden design, her hands sometimes clad in boxing gloves.

Wind, heat, cold, and disease took their toll on the old garden, as on the new, leaving ghost plants in their wake. Most impacted were the trees. Whether coniferous or deciduous, trees play an outsized role in the landscape, providing shade, carbon capture and wildlife habitat. Their loss can leave a gaping wound in garden and gardener alike.

My mom had always threatened to move if the city cut down the cedar in front of our house to widen the street. Her passion for trees, along with the fact that my dad had studied forestry, meant a love of trees was practically part of my DNA. So when my garden's Port Orford cedars, endemic to the southern Oregon coast, began to wither and brown like discarded Christmas trees, I grieved in earnest. The cedars all succumbed to a fungus, but the wood was put to good use, first as split-rail fencing, later as edging for our garden paths.

The most unexpected ghost maker was a summer lighting storm that set a neighbor's Douglas fir ablaze and shattered another neighbor's redwoods, sending shards the size of two-by-fours flying into our yard. The loss of those majestic trees and an incense cedar the neighbor deemed too messy, exposed us to the full heat of the western sun. The shade garden I'd planned along a dry creek bed became completely impractical. Even the drought tolerate, sun-loving plants that now grace that feature—rosemary, catmint, and sedums—suffered under a hopefully once-in-a-lifetime heat dome that stalled over the Pacific Northwest in 2021, sending temperatures to a record high 116 degrees. Our conifers, already stressed by drought, shed their needles like dogs with mange. The blueberries fried and the leaves of rhododendrons drooped in what can only be likened to utter despair.

Any despair I'd felt over losing our funky old house with its sloping floors, leaky windows and tenacious carpenter ants dissipated as the new structure began to take shape, guided by an architect willing to work on a small-scale project, just 1,500 square feet, and an easy-going contractor, a would-be cowboy fond of pointy-toed boots.

As much as the new house would shape the garden, the garden also shaped the house. We needed a floor plan that would fit our existing footprint so as not to impinge on the swath of lawn that contained the drain field. And the trees, too, were a consideration. We wanted to keep the ginkgo with its sudden display of golden leaves, and equally sudden leaf fall. We'd watched that tree grow from a sapling to a sturdy sentinel, a symbol of sorts for our enduring marriage. And the Oregon white oak, a stately old native that I'd viewed from my writing desk, became the inspiration for the skylight in the new dining room, its dark limbs often cradling the moon.

Other trees didn't fare so well. The pines, the lilacs, even the widowed pears had to go. Still, we saved what we could of the foundation plantings. A professional crew moved the old rhododendrons at the front of the house to new locations along the periphery, along with a weigela that had flirted with our gutter for years. I saved what I could, transplanting the honeysuckle to a bed beside the raspberry patch, digging up sword fern and iris, daylily and bergenia and heeling them into a shady spot as far from the construction as I could manage.

I'd like to say I had a well-thought-out design for the new garden, but my planning energies were exhausted by all the details required to build a house. Every door hinge, light fixture, and sink faucet had to be selected, along with windows, paint colors, counter tops, fireplace, and flooring. Finally, prodded by those pointy-toed boots, we added a landscape architect to the team. She helped us site two rain gardens and a dry creek bed, move in river rock and boulders, and design our gravel pathways.

By December, when the last nail-gun fell silent, we were able to move from our temporary rental just two blocks away to our brand new home, a home nestled among our stalwart old trees, but largely surrounded by bark dust spread to prevent erosion. Much of the soil around the new build was compacted and infertile, too cold and soggy to plant that winter, but come the spring, I couldn't wait to grab a shovel and break in a new pair of gardening gloves.

I'd never been gifted such a blank garden canvas, and found the task invigorating, if at times daunting. After countless hours browsing nurseries and searching the internet, I finally selected small flowering trees and shrubs that would support wildlife as well as provide much needed structure. Rose of Sharon, beauty bush, and red-veined enkianthus joined native high-bush cranberry, flowering currant, and Oregon grape, as well as rosemary, fuchsia, catmint, and an assortment of dwarf conifers inspired by the Oregon Garden's impressive collection. There were so many plants to choose from and so much space to fill that I succumbed to the one-of-these, one-of-those mentality typical of beginning gardeners. I should have known better, but the effect, if haphazard, fit the goal we'd set for the house as well—environmentally sound with a touch of whimsy.

Ten years on, I remain thankful for my garden, for the chance to shape and reshape it as the mood strikes or nature demands, even as I'm haunted by what the garden might become when I can no longer do it justice. But I have hope, too, specifically H.O.P.E. Oregon, a local non-profit with whom I volunteer. H.O.P.E. helps elders remain in their homes by providing community volunteers to prune, weed, mow, rake, clean gutters, or fix fences. Working in other people's gardens has given me a greater appreciation for my own, and an eye for what features might best endure. Knowing there's a chance, even a ghost of a chance that some part of my garden might survive me—a tree, a fern, a fragrant vine—I can sleep more soundly at night.

The Inspiration of Other Gardens

Suellen Cox

IN YOUR LIFE, WHAT has given you joy? What has inspired you? What has initiated a journey and sent you down paths you never expected to travel? During the past forty years, I have experienced unexpected joy admiring gardens in many places—California, Canada, France, Italy, and beyond. It was in Great Britain, however, that my gardening journey began. It was the gardens of two twentieth century British women: poet, novelist, and gardener Vita Sackville-West's Sissinghurst garden; and post-impressionist artist and gardener Vanessa Bell's garden at Charleston Farmhouse in Sussex. Both gardens provided joy and immense inspiration. My journey, and the pleasure of first creating gardens, and then creating art began with them and has led me down paths I never imagined I would travel.

When I was growing up in Whittier, California, I witnessed another woman, my mother, attempting to make our modest track home more pleasing by planting flowers: stately gladiolas and sweet peas that she trellised in a sunny spot next to our garage. At that time, and until my mid-thirties, I had not been bitten by the gardening bug.

It was in the late 1970s when my husband, daughter, and I moved to narrow Silverado Canyon in Southern California that the first inklings of a desire to "garden" was felt. We were a young family seeking to come together with like-minded others and a more natural way to live; a place where children could wade in creeks and climb old oaks. In moving to Silverado, one of several canyons in the Santa Ana

Mountains, we felt we had struck the illusive yet legendary silver vein that early prospectors had sought, and that had given the canyon its name. Within our first months I was delighted by the wild and rugged landscape, meandering creek, and abundant wildlife. For a few years we rented several houses with little yard before buying a creek-side house, small like a child's fist and square as a postage stamp. Sitting on a quarter acre populated by two oaks, a redwood, a towering sycamore, and a Santa Rosa plum tree, the house was also surrounded by good bones—old grey stone walls and pathways. Roused by the canyon's natural beauty, and remembering my mother's pleasure in the aroma of her sweet peas, I began to wonder, could I put in a few beds and grow her favorites?

As a 37-year-old mother of now two daughters, part-time library assistant, and later-in-life college student studying English literature, I discovered the writing of Virginia Woolf, and subsequently through her read Vita Sackville-West's poetry and novels. It was, however, the discovery of her books of garden writing—*Some Flowers* and *In Your Garden*—where inspiration bloomed for me. That blooming was heightened on a family trip to Great Britain in June 1987 when a visit was made to her Sissinghurst Castle and garden. The old stone castle was beautiful, but it was the orchard and outdoor garden rooms—the rose and the cottage garden that I fell for. Her famous "white garden" in summer was spectacular. Vita had an instinctive gift for planting; she was a romantic, and put that sense of romance into the flowers she planted profusely and with abandon. I was inspired. Was this—but on a much smaller scale—something, I could aspire to?

Over the next few years my attempts at creating a garden were hit and miss. I was a novice after all. I had to learn the difference between perennials and annuals, basics of watering, the importance of sun exposure. For example, in my canyon neighborhood I learned that due to narrow canyon walls, I had no direct sunlight hitting my garden until late March. This was a challenge I needed to work with. I learned that because of the higher elevation, the canyon experienced more pronounced seasons than the "flat lands" of Orange County. The Matilija poppies withered in the summer heat. Sycamore leaves turned flaming yellow and red in the fall. It was usually colder in winter—it sometimes snowed—and was warmer in summer. We could get torrential rainstorms in winters, like boxer's gloves pummeling the peaks and canyon walls for days on end, invariably leading to quickly rising and swiftly moving creeks. These issues were challenging and informed my learning and my gardening efforts. On a more positive note, the canyon's plant diversity and nearby residents' interests could be a real advantage. One year after obtaining horse manure from a canyon neighbor's horse corral and spreading it in a spot in my garden, I let it rest, then planted sweet pea seeds. I was later rewarded with a glorious display of the most fragrant sweet peas!

Around this time, I and my friend Patty, also a novice gardener, had been hiking in the Cleveland National Forest that surrounds Silverado. We became familiar with the canyon's flora and fauna. We were amazed at the abundant growth of California natives in spring on sunny slopes and shaded areas by streams. We decided it might be interesting to experiment with growing California natives on a small spit of land adjacent to my home. We started in the fall as that is the best time to plant California natives in Southern California. This fall planting allows winter rains to get the roots of plants well established. We had our own strengths in this effort: Patty loved sitting with a pencil and paper laying out a detailed plan of the plants we most admired, and what should be planted in shady as well as sunny spots. Me, I just wanted to get my hands dirty, dig in the dirt, and plant seeds and one-gallon plants with abandon. We visited numerous nurseries in Southern California that grew and sold California native plants and seeds: Tree of Life Nursery in San Juan Capistrano and Theodore Payne in Sun Valley. We also visited and found inspiration at the 86-acre Rancho Santa Ana Botanic Gardens in Claremont, now known as the California Botanic Garden, whose goal is to advance knowledge, conservation, and appreciation of California natives. We learned which plants grew fast and tall, which stayed small and compact, and which reseeded.

After coming up with a plan, this neglected "spit" of land required a lot of physical labor. Weeds and downed tree limbs were cleared, an old cement mixer moved and a sign posted "Free for the taking," small rocks and large boulders unearthed, and the soil turned. All was accomplished over a period of several weekends. What was then planted? A California red-bud, Mexican flannelbush, Ceanothus, baby blue eyes, California blue-eyed grass, sticky monkeyflower, Iris douglasiana, yellow bush poppy, salvias, California poppies, and others. We patiently waited for the winter rains, and impatiently for flowers to bloom. In the spring of that year the native garden was glorious. What did this teach me? That with a good dose of inspiration, a dear friend to lend ideas and elbow grease, and patience, much could be accomplished. My native garden did not look like Vita's Sissinghurst garden, but it was no less beautiful, and more importantly, it was appropriate for the canyon climate, drought tolerant, and sustainable. This experiment had been a success. However, I felt there was still so much I didn't know.

Always one for life-long learning, I, along with another friend Andrea, registered to take an Orange County Master Gardner's course. During the four-month, once a week class, we learned research-based knowledge on home horticulture: plant pathology; soils; composting; growing vegetables, flowers, fruit and landscape trees; water quality, irrigation and conservation; pests and plant problems. This course was invaluable in my growth as a gardener.

By this time, between part-time library work, college coursework, and mother's work, my reading journey with the works of Vita Sackville-West and significantly Virginia Woolf, had evolved. I was now reading the diaries and biographies. It was through these that I became acquainted with Woolf's elder sister Vanessa Bell. I then read Francis Spaulding's biography of her, and Regina Marler's *Selected Letters of Vanessa Bell*. To say I was now entirely smitten with Bell's work and life is an understatement. She became my muse.

Bell is probably best known as Woolf's sister. However, above all she was a prolific painter and leading figure in early twentieth century, post-impressionist British art. A wife, devoted mother, and practical gardener, she is also known for the country home and garden she created in the Sussex countryside, Charleston Farmhouse, from 1916 until her death in 1961. A must-see destination for art lovers and gardeners, Charleston is now open to the public and draws thousands of visitors from across the world each year.

I first visited Charleston in 2000 and was entirely enchanted. The house itself is a work of art where every available surface—walls, doors, furniture, cupboards, and screens—is painted on. Unfortunately, when I visited in early April, the garden, with the exception of lemon-yellow daffodils, was mostly dormant. The good bones of the flint walled garden, the graveled pathways, and the mosaiced small pond did provide a dramatic background and sense of artistry at work and things to come.

When I returned in 2002 for a week-long Charleston Summer Workshop, the late June garden was a riot of color, attractive shapes, and lovely fragrance. It was in its glory. The kitchen garden showed its abundance with burgundy wine-colored plums, green broad beans, and globe artichokes. The borders were ablaze with hundreds of flower species: zinnias, delphiniums, and sunflowers to name a few; and of course, Bell's personal favorite—towering hollyhocks in jewel-tone colors. The perfumed roses were intoxicating. It was truly a "painters" garden. I have returned to Charleston Farmhouse on other occasions and am always inspired.

Although Bell's Charleston garden never ceases to be a source of inspiration, when it comes to my own gardens, I have had to be especially creative and apply that inspiration to more practical matters like local environments, micro-climates, soil composition, and dealing with California's droughts. My native garden, and the Master Gardener course, provided important lessons concerning the matters above, that I then applied when turning to the sparse borders and beds surrounding my own house. Many of Charleston's flowers were not appropriate for my property. I had success with some perennials but not all. Sometimes I would buy plants that caught my eye, plant them, and they wouldn't thrive. Bell especially favored red flowers and taller varieties of plants; they didn't work in my garden. Whether due to the canyon light, the gray stone walls, or the color, and low-slung nature of the house, I found that varying shades of pink, purple, and ivory flowers as well as smaller shrubs, provided a more pleasing palette to the eye. Roses like "white iceberg shrub" grew better than more intense sun-loving roses. Purple iris, coral bells, alstroemeria, meadow rue, campanulas, and Iceland poppies all seemed to do well in the filtered sunlight in spring. Also, due to the success with California natives, I introduced a few natives here in sunnier spots. Various varieties of salvias thrived, especially salvia waverly, and clevelandii.

In creating my two canyon gardens I learned so much, and they were flourishing. During the years 2008 – 2012, my gardens were on several Southern California spring garden tours: The Mary Lou Heard Memorial Tour and the Modjeska/Silverado Canyons Garden Tour. Over two weekend days in 2009, over 400 people visited. Those numbers increased in 2010 and 2012. Each year there was a great deal of work to be done getting ready for those spring tours, and there were always nagging questions a month before: will my gardens be ready, will the Cécile Brünner be at its peak, will the weather cooperate or will we have early May showers? It was such a joy welcoming friends, neighbors, and other garden lovers to my gardens, answering questions, and sharing gardening tips. After one tour, several artists asked to paint various views of my gardens. Of course, I said yes. I've always appreciated this quote by Richard Wright in his book *The Gardener's Bed-Book*: "Gardening should be done in blinders. Its distractions are tempting and persistent, and only by stern exercise of will do I ever finish one job without being lured off to another." For several days the painters were at their easels, and I went discreetly about being lured from first one job to another: dead-heading roses, watering, and harvesting herbs.

Around this time, in addition to gardening I was learning to utilize emerging online technologies into my professional life as an academic librarian: designing and producing library research web guides and blogging. I took a campus workshop on creating blogs that would give me the basics. As a trial run I decided to create a blog on something that I was passionate about—gardening! Blogging my Silverado garden's seasons in words and pictures taught me a lot about online design and it turned into a multi-year project. I incorporated gardening quotes by well-known gardeners such as Gertrude Jekyll and Vita Sackville-West; and also writers—Virginia Woolf and Katherine Mansfield; and artists—Vanessa Bell. I posted photographs that I took showing the seasons: snow on the ground in winter; the first blossoms on the plum tree in early spring; perennials struggling in August heat; the glorious red and gold leaves on the trellised California wild grape in late fall. Blogging was an excellent way of documenting not only what was being planted and growing in the changing seasons, but also my continuing evolution as a gardener.

In October 2007, a fire swept through the canyons. It had been a dry year: sagebrush was brittle; the brown hills parched like tender. When Santa Ana winds blow, inevitably fires erupt. Fires will have their way: they scorn boundaries; respect no fences; mock efforts to be contained. This fire was no different. It grew larger, the menacing winds continually shifting. The canyons were placed under mandatory evacuations. We evacuated. Soon, eight residential structures were damaged and six destroyed in Modjeska and Williams Canyon. Helicopters were called in to scoop up water from Irvine Lake and douse the hillside flames in rotating shifts. Strike-teams of over 200 firefighters and 100 fire engines were now in Silverado, their orders—to protect homes. Planes were called in to dump fire retardant on homes in immediate danger—ours included. Later the winds shifted again moving the flames away from Silverado. Cooler temperatures helped the fire-fighting efforts. In Silverado, no homes were lost. However, many of us were as emotionally scarred as the physically scarred oaks on canyon ridgelines, and sycamores along Santiago Canyon Road. For me, during this time of raging fires, the anxiety and fear, the possibility of losing this community, our home and gardens was intense. I began searching online for canyon-like areas and small homes in Northern California where my daughter and son-in-law lived and were planning to start a family. I was looking forward to grandchildren someday. Searching was my way of coping, of seeing a future. When the fire was eventually contained and evacuation lifted, we were told we could return to our homes. Driving into the canyon I didn't know what to expect. In several areas it looked like a moonscape. Driving along Silverado Canyon Road, sumac, sage, and once bright yellow Spanish broom that had once hugged the sides of the road had all been swept away by flames. Our tiny local post office, library, and Canyon market though empty, were still standing. Arriving at our property, the gate to my garden was open. Ash was everywhere. Phos-Chek fire retardant gel covered the house, windows, and much of both gardens. I unlocked the front door and walked in. I was home.

My gardens had survived. We lived five more years in Silverado and I continued to garden. I watched the seasons come and go, but something had shifted. Our first granddaughter was born. Being nearer to family became a priority. When looking for our next home in the Bay Area, a desired requirement was a garden or potential for a garden. We looked for, and eventually found, a house on half an acre in Orinda. We moved.

The property had good bones—hardscape, mature trees and plants, and potential for raised vegetable beds. Some elements of this Orinda garden were similar to Silverado. There was a Santa Rosa plum, two large oaks, and a redwood. There were also differences. In addition to several Japanese maples, there were apple trees, a pear, three lemon and two orange trees. There was more sun exposure. Established rhododendrons of different varieties and colors grew in shadier areas and under two wooden pergolas. Slowly, I began making changes, making this garden my own. To make it more sustainable I added drought tolerant plants—salvias, rosemary, and Santa Barbara daisy. These added to the garden's diversity. I also contended with certain challenges: more clay soil; marauding squirrels in the vegetable beds; a colder climate in winter; and I was in my late sixties and physically not able to garden for hours on end.

As my Orinda garden evolved and flourished, so did I. In order to memorialize my Silverado Canyon blog, I turned it into a book. I also created another blog—*Leaves and Blooms: Musings on My Garden and Life Inspired by Virginia, Vita, and Vanessa*. My creative juices began flowing towards art. I was taking what I had learned as a gardener—composition, scale, color, form, and texture—and applying it to making collages assemblage, and, most importantly, artist's books. This became my passion.

I still garden daily, whether dead-heading my white iceberg roses, tending my fruit trees, or pruning back orange clock vine. But more often, you will find me in my studio imagining possibilities, exploring new techniques, and creating my art. It has been a journey down paths I never expected to travel, and it all began with the inspiration of other gardens.

The Forest as Garden

Deborah Fleming

THE VALLEY VIEW SPUR of the Shagbark Woods, off a narrow gravel lane in Richland County, Ohio, is easy to miss. I discovered it when invited to a hike in July 2021, led by Eric, trustee of the North Central Ohio Land Conservancy, which seeks to conserve intact ecosystems. The land encompasses 172 acres of old-growth forest donated by a farmer named Hammond.

A sign at the entrance to the woods exhorted hikers to stay on the marked path because the vegetation was fragile. Nearby, an abandoned, nineteenth-century brick schoolhouse loomed in shadows. Restored or not, ruins retain romanticism that no modern building ever achieves and remind us that whatever civilization we are born into will be replaced by another; at the same time, we can never entirely undo what has been done.

We were joined by a naturalist who wore black elastic hiking pants, long sleeves, and gloves in spite of midsummer heat. Our naturalist companion pulled up stems and stuffed them into his backpack while Eric narrated the ecological history of the place. The woods include many trees older than 200 years and more than eighty feet high, among them red and white oak, red and sugar maple, tulip tree, shagbark hickory, and other species. Seedlings sprouted from the leaf-strewn forest floor along with midsummer-blooming jewelweed, blazing star, and blue vervain (Latin *verbena*, "sacred plant"). Fallen trees, necessary for official designation as old growth forest by the Ohio Division of Forestry, are allowed to decay into "nursery logs" where lichens survive along with insects and grubs which attract birds. Monarch butterflies clustered around some shrubs. Spring blossoms had faded into brown petals, but the forest was not the "diminished thing" of Robert Frost's poem of the ovenbird and its summer habitat.

Invasive plants account for more than 40% of the decline in threatened and endangered species. Our guide scouted for the most intrusive of all—garlic mustard, so-called for the smell produced when its leaves are crushed—which has become particularly destructive in the temperate climates of the Northeast and Midwest. Hikers and gardeners are familiar with *Alliaria petiolata*'s dark green, toothed leaves and diminutive white flowers. Brought from Europe in the 1800s for medicinal uses and erosion control, it spreads seeds on the wind. Emerging early in the spring, it crowds out native plants, releases chemicals that alter the underground network of fungi that convey nutrients to roots, and ultimately inhibits sapling survival. Although it is easy to pull out because of its tap root, getting rid of it sometimes requires years.

Another invasive, called Tree of Heaven, does not transform these woods into paradise. The genus name, *Ailanthus*, comes from the Indonesian language Ambonese and means "the tree that reaches for the sky"; the species name, *altissima*, is Latin for "tallest." Distinguished from the native sumac, ash, and black walnut by its reddish-brown twigs and smooth-edged leaves, Tree of Heaven, unlike other species of *Ailanthus*, thrives not in tropical but in temperate climates and was grown in China as a host for the *ailanthus* silkmoth, which produces a sturdier fabric than the silkworm. In the 1740s, merchants and Jesuit missionaries brought what they called the "Chinese sumac" to Europe where it gained popularity among gardeners because of its rapid growth, shadiness, and resistance to plant disease.

Another invasive that inhibits native species and is named for a cultural myth is the burning bush (*Euonymus alatus*), imported from northeast Asia in 1860 as an ornamental. For about three weeks in the autumn its flame-red leaves are spectacular, but during most of the year it is unattractive, with dark, drab-green leaves and scraggly, gray-brown branches. While it is called a shrub, it can grow to ten feet in height and five or more in width, sometimes becoming unwieldy in gardens and lawns. In forests, its seeds dropped or disseminated by birds prevent other species from surviving. In the story (Exodus 3:2–6), from a flaming bush, God instructed Moses to lead his people into a promised land. No miracle today, perhaps the burning bush speaks to us of migration and a persistent belief that somewhere there exists an ideal place as some of the original colonists hoped when they sailed to what they called "the new world."

Jacob's Ladder (*Polemonium vanbruntiae*), also a midsummer flower named for the biblical narrative, is indigenous although endangered. A member of the phlox family and woodland perennial, it grows as high as three feet and has pointed leaves and, in summer, clusters of bell-shaped, bluish-purple flowers that attract pollinators. Paired leaflets are said to resemble the ladder to heaven that appeared in a dream to the patriarch Jacob, son of Isaac and grandson of Abraham (Genesis 28:12). Whatever its symbolism, the plant fares best in shady places with organic soils in the Northeast, but once established, it is tolerant both of drought and deer.

We noticed dried grasses in the xylem confluence of trees that looked like birds' nests; they turned out to be piles of invasive grasses pulled up and left to dry until the seeds are dead. Volunteers then drop them onto the trail to help prevent soil erosion. Caretakers' work was evident: where non-native species had been eliminated, wild orchids and other colorful woodland flowers grew in abundance. The arboreal confluence used to be called a "crotch": nomenclature thus represents our bodies' relationship to the land, or perhaps merely reveals a pathetic fallacy.

Eric explained that horizontal lines like crosscut saw marks high on the trunks of white oak and tulip trees were the work of yellow-bellied sapsuckers whose pecking allows sticky juice to flow from inner to outer layers of the bark. Insects attracted to the ooze become stuck and make protein-rich meals for the woodpeckers. According to Douglas Tallamy in *The Nature of Oaks*, white oaks sustain four thousand species of animals, birds, and insects. By contrast, the burning bush plays host to aphids, black weevils, and spider mites along with the euonymus caterpillar (*Yponomeuta cagnagella*) which, like its host, is a colonizer.

"Insects, not people, control the world," Eric commented.

Early in the hike I spied what I guessed were tiny floating pin feathers from birds, but as I observed them, realized that they must be living, as they did not fall to the ground but propelled themselves through the air like swimmers. Someone speculated that they must be moths.

We crossed an old farm lane and saw first-hand the result of disturbance: multiflora rose growing profusely; no large trees or nursery logs. Fence posts with box wire still attached testified that the area had once been pasture. A few meters farther and we were in old growth again, although younger than the previous section of truly ancient inhabitants. In this section sugar maples dominated. Volunteers had laid sticks, called "dry dams," horizontally across slopes to impede soil erosion from rainwater.

In another section, slender stalks of common alumroot were now "common" again. Before the systematic removal of invasives, volunteers counted twenty Canada lilies; in 2020, they counted 300. Northern maidenhair fern spread profusely along the path, a threatened indigenous species that grows only in mature forests. One area nicknamed "Dutchman's bowl" formed a swale where Dutchman's breeches, an indigenous plant whose pantaloon-shaped white flowers bloom only in dense woods, now thrive. We saw forest flame, or forest candelabra flowers, and we spotted a Luna moth (*Actias luna*). Its celadon-green wings with purple "fringe" and four "eyes" (colored spots) spread as wide as a person's palm. Although in the same family with the Asiatic silkworm, they are not closely related, and their cocoons do not produce the fine fibers of the Asian moth. They belong to the family called *Saturniidae* for Saturn, Roman god of time, generation, abundance, and renewal. Usually active at night, they are now endangered due to pesticide use and habitat loss. Thus, they are not abundant and their renewal today depends not on the will of the gods but on the will of human beings to preserve woodlands.

High in the trees I could hear a willow flycatcher, invisible because of the dense canopy.

Later I investigated the mystery of the tiny moths and learned they were probably nearly microscopic creatures called woolly alder aphids (*Prociphilus tessellatus*), smaller than a half centimeter. Also termed "fairy flies," they produce fluffy white colonies that look like cotton candy on tree branches and suck phloem from leaves, producing a sticky substance called "honeydew." A sooty mold fungus then often colonizes the residue and produces a dense black fuzzy mat. In the fall, this layer becomes spongy and yellow and is sometimes mistaken for arboreal disease when the only real damage is aesthetic. Woolly alder aphids and their relations maple blight aphids cause no harm to overall health of trees but are prey for lacewings, hoverflies, lady beetles, and parasitic wasps which also feed on garden pests such as Japanese beetles, mites, melon aphids, and cabbage worms. Never before had I noticed the woolly aphids, perhaps because their tiny white wings, which appear iridescent in the darkness under a high canopy, were invisible in abundant light in fields and younger woods. I learned to see them in shadows, not in radiance.

These fairy-like creatures remind me that although human beings in our hubris or narcissism tell ourselves that the world is an unending resource created for us, most of the evidence points in the opposite direction: both the complexity of the biosphere and the unimaginable size of the universe reveal our infinitesimal unimportance. The vast majority of earthly creatures take no notice of us unless we destroy their habitat. Some Native American groups believed animals to be their greatest teachers because non-human species know instinctively how to survive, whereas people must be painstakingly taught and of all mammals are the slowest to mature. If one definition of wisdom is humility, then perhaps the greatest lesson we can learn is that we should be glad to be only a tiny part of the infinite beauty, much of which is yet to be known.

In the United States, while the national parks represent the impulse to protect "wilderness" as we conceive of it, state parks protect natural areas on a smaller scale. The 120-acre Doris Duke Woods at Malabar Farm State Park contain red and white oak, beech, sugar maple, shagbark hickory, aspen, tulip poplar, and a few eastern hemlock. Saplings and ferns thrive around rocky sandstone outcroppings. Visiting in late summer, I heard the hammering of woodpeckers, shriek of a red-tailed hawk, and long shrill notes of the wood pee-wee. From a safe distance, chipmunks chattered at me. Orange forget-me-not, pink lady's thumb, yellow wild snapdragons, horseweed, snakeroot, ragweed, coneflowers, primrose, curly dock, Japanese knotweed, white blazing star (also called fairy wand), and bird's-foot trefoil still bloomed, although the beautiful purple blossoms of great lobelia were fading.

Near the pathways I saw profusions of American feverfew, green stems perhaps two feet high with pointed leaves and clusters of tiny white flowers. *Parthenium* obtains its genus name from the Greek word for "virgin;" the Parthenon temple on the Acropolis is dedicated to Athena, goddess of wisdom, revered for her chastity. The species name *integrifolium* comes from Latin and means "uncut." The plant's medicinal properties inspired the common names "feverfew" and "wild quinine": it was once used to cure fever or headaches. Today we rely on manufacturers for healing drugs and have largely forgotten what our ancestors knew of the power of wild plants. I do not suggest giving up miraculous drugs developed over the last century but learning to appreciate what quietly grows unbidden around us and not losing the old knowledge.

Sacred trees and forests occupy an important place in legend and myth. Sometimes deep woods are associated with danger, chaos, savagery, lawlessness, or loss of individuality; conversely, they represent freedom, innocence, safety from corruption, and affirmation of personality. The Garden of Eden contained many trees from which the human inhabitants might freely eat but also the tree of forbidden knowledge. A tree—we are not told what kind—becomes the cross. The Greek goddess Artemis, patron of the grove, never appeared to human beings. Dionysus, god of vegetation, wine, and revelry, who was also hanged on a tree, gave his name to primal emotions. In Norse mythology, the ash Yggdrasil stood at the center of the world below which flowed springs of destiny, wisdom, and understanding. The god Odin hung from its branches for nine days and nights in order to acquire hidden knowledge. Ancient druids associated oak trees with wisdom and hazel trees with creativity and inspiration. The word "tree" in Indo-European stems from the same root as "true:" *dreu*; in Anglo-Saxon, the word *treow* contains both meanings.

Another cultural myth begins with a garden of paradise and the first human being naming all the plants and animals, although we do not know what language he spoke, why he chose the names he did, or which were his favorites. Perhaps he represents an archetype of each tribe or clan which must find names for the creatures they encounter in their environment as biologists create universal names from languages thought to be "dead." Perhaps we need a new, nature-centered myth or a new understanding of the old myth to provide the foundation for a way of life that might ensure survival of the biosphere as we know and depend on it. It may be that we have already arrived at the Promised Land and failed to recognize it.

Ecce Homo [Sexual] Ad Hortus Conclusus

Olumayowa Anjolaoluwa Willoughby

I.
I am solo-traveling. Not that this is any different than any other moment or any other person in any other life . . . so I guess . . . I am solo-traveling . . . too? Or again. Or rather again and again. No. Solo-traveling strange? Solo-traveling strangely. Yes. I am solo-traveling strangely again and again. I am working on different farms and in different gardens through World Wide Opportunities on Organic Farms (WOOFing) staying with different warm hearts. Loves. Families. Providing company and love and laughs in exchange for food to eat and a place to sleep. Ballin' on a budget. Bawlin on a budget? Bawlin and on a budget. Or maybe just bawlin . . .

II.
I am listening to FKA Twigs on repeat these days. "Water Me" has been my daily soundtrack for healing and growth and restoration:

> "He told me I was so small. I told him water me."

I didn't realize how much of this WOOFing experience would be about my experience with white people experiencing their experience. I mean I imagined white people would be in these spaces but I didn't anticipate my day to day being so informed by their mere existence. By the things that surprise them. The things that intrigue them. The things that make them laugh. I mean, my GOD. And the ways they talk amongst each other and try and make sense of it all is like watching something really sad and really infuriating at the same time. It is rather overwhelming. Right now there are two white boys from Belgium, a white family from Switzerland, a white woman from Slovakia and a young man that arrived from Brazil yesterday afternoon (lol at Brazilian race politics Brazil being complicated). They are all very nice people. We laugh. We work together. We high five. And yet I drown hours of conversation out because the details are too fucked up for me to endure. One trick I have learned though is, because I am considered the single English expert since white girl left, to say "Oh in English, [insert thing] is considered fucked up." Even if the thing has nothing to do with the language and everything to do with the idea. Lol. "Oh, we don't pull our eyes into slits and say 'Orientals' in English because it's offensive." "Oh, in English it makes sense to think of a nation as multifaceted because history happened already and to say someone does or doesn't 'look' [insert nationality] implies nationhood is inherent rather than historically circumscribed." And people are like oh. Okay. Lol. There are just so many thoughts and so many feelings that run through my head and my heart in any given moment. I feel like I am here to "experience rural life." Like I am paying to get my "rural fix." These animals, all in cages, are here so that we can get the experience of a good rural Thai town. And the Thai people that live here in Chat pa wai are part of the package deal. COME ONE COME ALL AND EXPERIENCE THE CHAT PA WAI ZOO. COWS, SHEEP, DOGS, AND THAI PEOPLE ALL INCLUDED. And it really really bothers me. I didn't come for the experience of it all. I came because I thought I was helping on a farm and learning how to grow things. The animals on this farm are not eaten, they are not sold for profit, they are just held. In a pen. For us to be changed and have a better life. Kind of like POC at a PWI. I have learned in five days what it took me four years to see: All animals exist for the benefit of white people everywhere. And this, this hurts. Today I worked more in the garden and I felt really good about that. I love working with plants. I love watering and planting and watching things grow. I hear FKA Twigs constantly in my head with every swing of my hoe. We water the small things if we want them to grow. I wonder how these white people see me. I wonder how these white people see the people of Chat Pa Wai. If they think about us and how big and beautiful we are. How we all need nurturing to grow. If they want us to be anything but small.

III.
i thought working on gardens, putting hand to earth, learning what it looks like to green and grow would heal me. but then there were those times there wasn't enough water. and then there were those times the water was too much. and the mint in the shade grew bigger and fuller than the mint in the sun because would you look at that, the mint prefers the shade. and who knew sometimes the sun can be a bit too bright. take a bit too much out of us. in Cyprus whose little green and purple things with the orange lining are weeds but here in Palestine I learned they have the highest concentration of Omega 3 fatty acids of any living thing in the world. and maybe things are only weeds sometimes in some places in the wrong kind of light. and we scoff and we uproot but never tested for all its promise. and i don't know where i am going with this. i don know where i am going at all but i thought laying w these plants would heal me and it's my fault for putting so much pressure on a few xylem and phloem but it's okay cause these days . . . i'm just trying to heal myself.

IV.
When I die bury me in my garden. bare. no casket. give me back to the earth that has given me so much. let flowers bloom on top of me. watch as trees spring up, casting shadows. eat their fruits. pick the flowers. say a prayer.
ashes to ashes; dust to dust.

V.
My dad and I aren't close. Growing up, he was present physically. And though physical presence is often used as the metric of good/

bad fatherhood, I have learned quite intimately that there is more than one way to be absent. A professor once explained to me that there is a whole generation of West African men who have made horrible fathers. The way it's been theorized is that many West African men who came of age during times of liberation have really contentious relationships with masculinity because of how colonization was deeply rooted in emasculation. After a professor had finished explaining this to me, I sat and cried for a really long time. My father was ten when Nigeria gained its independence from Britain. Maybe we never stood a chance. My relationship with my mother has always been really different from my relationship with my father. Yorubas generally trace lineage through the father's geography but I'd never say I was from my dad's Lagos. It's my mother's Ibadan for me. It's a place I've only been once but in things relating to my mother I have always felt homed. In 1985 my parents got married. Two years later they had my older sister. When my sister was two years old, they packed up everything they could carry, left everything they knew and moved to the United States of America. I was borne on the other side of the Atlantic. My parents blame many things on this fact. In 2012 I was outed as queer by the radical leftist newspaper for which I wrote. It was at this time I also became an abomination to my mother and father. I have spent the past three years trying to understand my parents better. I have this theory that if I can make sense of their disapproving glances, their deep sighs, their head shakes, and harsh words I can better understand myself? Maybe it makes no sense at all. Or maybe it makes too much sense. Regardless, it's a project I have committed myself to fully. I have found, in recent years, similarities to this project that resonate with earthwork. Till, plant, repeat. I have given myself over to such processes. There is something about sending one's energies, one's whole self into a life energy, into its desires, its intricacies, its deep sighs and disapproving glances and hoping to God it will peek its head from the soily dark matter and say yes to the expounding possibilities under the sun. My mom has said yes quite a bit in the past three years. I used to think it was her love for me that was helping her work through her inability to understand me, her daughter, born in another time, in another country, Q-U-E-E-R (my god anything but that). Now, I'm not so sure. My father prefers the soily dark matter. As much as it pains me, I think I understand. It doesn't talk back. It doesn't speak in foreign tongue. It doesn't demand stretching the heart and beating the mind into submission. It's comforting. It's predictable. I worry though that if he stays there, he will rot and that somehow I am already rotting with him.

The title of the essay translates to Behold the Gay in the Enclosed Garden. "Ecce Homo" are the Latin words used by Pontius Pilate, when he presents a scourged Jesus, bound and crowned with thorns, to a hostile crowd shortly before his crucifixion. It translates to "Behold, the Man."

Down and Dirty

Elizabeth Brulé Farrell

I AM IN THE middle of a bleak New England winter. Steel grey is the prominent color of the sky. Overnight a fresh snow fell, so this morning the garden is covered in white. There is a truth that touches me while looking out my window, how everything gets buried beneath it. There is no evidence of roots that sprawled below the surface where carrots and leeks begin to grow, or even evidence of the rabbit that would burrow deep to birth babies and emerge to nibble at the romaine and red lettuce come spring. All of that is lodged in memory as though far away from any realm of real experience, like a ghost garden hidden under the snow.

I buried my own ghosts, too, in the roots of events that shaped my life, longing to live free from the drink. Alcoholism plunged me into isolation and redirected my ambitions that also existed in unseen layers. This is more than a metaphor. Sipping my third cup of coffee, I allow myself to remember what it was like before I decided to imagine possibility.

In the late afternoon I brushed away snow with my bare hands, then lifted the protective garden fabric made to keep in heat, and found curly leaf parsley. Somehow this small discovery rendered within me a curious kind of hope, a kind of reassuring resilience that I wanted, too. Tenderly I picked it with my chilly wet fingers, elated to taste it, an elixir for all that ailed me. There is much that I could regret from past actions in the active period of my addiction, but it is the present that I want to bring to the forefront of what excites me. A few steps from the garden is the work shed where I haphazardly wished that maybe the potted rosemary might make it through the winter, as I wondered if I would also make it through. Placed behind the big glass door, it benefited from the sunlight when nature blessed it with infrequent visits. It still stood, romantically alluring to me, sturdy wooden stalks with an outreach of needle-like leaves. I took its survival as a generous invitation to snip several branches, an almost magical moment of simple bliss. It would infuse the house with its scent steeped in a vegetable broth with the parsley, the base of an intoxicating soup.

To be intoxicated takes on another meaning for me. Once to arrive in that condition, it was a liquid swallowed in a kind of disappointment and disillusion, a poison I poured into myself that put me in a self-made prison of mind and body. How incredible that something as simple as a garden could begin a long restoration process that would continue through the years and sustain a season-to-season enthusiasm. One day to the next is different, and demanding, and worth the muscle and energy put into it. I had wanted to become a sober woman and peacefully surrender to the unpredictability of life. It was what I wanted to plant and nurture. The slow intertwining of recovery and gardening brought back aspects of myself that I had long abandoned. It evolved into a continuum of joyful effort.

How the garden is doing is partly the environment: days of rain or sun, using seaweed as a mulch or building a compost pile from eggshells, peels, and coffee grounds that break down and create rich soil. So many daily decisions that required attention and were constantly changing as I was changing as well.

The history of taking care of the garden is the history of taking care of me. In my younger years, it made my body strong and showed me I had endurance. Working long hours and staying out until twilight thrilled me. I enjoyed the well-earned sweat, the cold rain that soaked my shirt.

I did not have many limitations then, but as I aged, and matured in my sobriety, I had to look at the reality of what lugging rocks to build a creeping thyme path did to my back. It caused me to reevaluate my physical ability. Initially noticing the loss, I lamented and lost interest in what used to bring pleasure and an abundant harvest to my table and psyche. I gradually turned away from it like a lover, not wanting the relationship anymore. Or so I made myself believe. The longer I turned my back on it, the more distraught I felt.

Bereft, I lingered in that place far too long. I thought if I cannot garden the way I did in my young womanhood, then I cannot garden at all. It was an all or nothing thinking, a black and white view. Like in my program of recovery, I started to grasp the idea of something in the middle. I needed to find new ways to reenter what once provided a daily routine that stabilized my moods and gave me purpose, a reason to check the weather and put on work clothes as my fashion of choice. I allowed myself to dream again.

The seed catalogues began to fill the mailbox. Lovely watercolor drawings of exquisite zucchini, pole beans, golden cherry tomatoes. A plethora of herbs said to have medicinal cures intrigued me. Angelica and borage, mugwort and horehound. I was being led into a wild garden of mind, diving into a period of being reinvigorated, a convalescence if you will. It came to me like the hand of a healer I did not know I needed.

There were setbacks, of course. One season I wrongly attacked the phlox. Neither well nor sick I was simply responding to living life on life's terms as the jargon of fellowship suggests, and bloodied my fingers pulling out plants, each stem feeling like a hair plucked from my scalp in a temporary madness, carnage of a long grieving process of losing my old life and forming a new one. Long into the darkness, beneath the beacon of moonlight, I worked to repair the undeserved damage I had caused the flowers. I prayed over them, that maybe one of them might forgive me and live, and some of them did.

I would bring a renewed attitude and spirit returning to the garden. Visiting the nursery, I took delight in watching older women who appeared energetic, though slower in step. There was eager banter about fertilizer and gloves and the supply of kneeling benches that had just arrived. This caught my attention. I approached them chatting in a circle over plants thriving in various sized clay and plastic pots and began asking them questions. Their wonderful words were a balm to me. They showed me how the kneeling bench worked and told me how it helped them garden with less pain. It also turned over to be a sitting bench and they lauded the necessary pauses in the tasks of weeding and poking holes in the ground with a finger, the right size for certain seeds. I left with a supply of beneficial tools. I bought the bench and thinner gloves for better gripping of the dreaded weeds that nearly suffocated the creeping thyme path. I wanted to save it. I wanted to go forward and not give up. I had come too far.

The few adaptive tools helped me think about what my body needed to participate in the garden again. I found that what the nursery women shared with me worked. It restored my desire to get dirty. Using the bench brought me low to the ground and was much easier than bending down with osteoporosis and arthritis. I found once more the pleasure of pruning lavender while listening to the symphony of the bees close to my ear. I rediscovered the sensuality of becoming flat on my back when I needed a break, the soft grass as my mattress, the sun warming my bones, unbuttoning my shirt to prolong the caress.

My days became organized around the garden chores, finding a resource within me I thought gone. Filling the car with the smell of plants selected to feed the eye and appetite, I felt rich in choices. The days were slower compared to what I used to accomplish quickly, but in taking my time it also slowed my too busy mind. It became a meditation to focus on one plant at a time, checking its leaves for mildew, aphids, wilting, or even having to pull out one that did not make it. I appreciated the cycle of life I was privileged to experience, for that is what it became: a privilege.

I planted marigolds for power. The faithful in Mexico, where I once attended the Day of the Dead rituals, scatter the flowers over streets and cemeteries, make garlands, and adorn altars with them. I was attracted to the lore of how their scent calls back the dead. All summer I carried buckets of water, tended them with a delicate and fervent longing, watched for buds to open and reveal themselves, as

I was revealing more of myself. Each day the garden and I were companions in growth and change I had not allowed myself to believe might happen. I thought those days were over.

At October's end, a sudden burst of pungent petals appeared. I placed them in vases throughout the house, set the table, and waited for the hungry ghosts I was ready to welcome back without fear. The positive woman I was before picking up the drink still existed but had been buried in alcohol like the garden in snow. Brushing away the layers that revealed the living parsley under its protective cover showed me to look at myself with the same curiosity. No longer in a place of hesitation about aging or my past destructive habits, I could embrace being a sober woman and a gardener once more.

Before the final harvest is complete, I pick the last tomato from the vine, pull up the leeks and shake the dirt free from their roots. No mourning what is nearly done. Spring will come again, and so will my happiness for what it brings.

Florilegium

Roxanne Lien

FLORILEGIUM COMES FROM THE Latin words Flore (flowers) and Legere (to gather and collect). I've gathered the following Flore anthologies from my journals, hoping to create a bouquet for those who love the art of gardening.

By nature, I'm a daydreamer, animal lover, traveler, reader, and writer, but above all, I am a gardener. Being a gardener in Minnesota is not always easy and is often filled with challenges, disappointments, and lessons learned the hard way. Nevertheless, I have been a gardener for 56 of my 72 years. I'm both bewitched and enchanted by nature, marveling at what one tiny seed can do. The wonders of nature have affected how I see the world, the stories I write, and how often it can clear away the cobwebs of my mind.

FLORE I: NELLIE'S GARDEN

When I retired at 52, I bought a small farm in the Sheyenne National grasslands of North Dakota—the 1880s homestead was known locally as Nellie's Place. Besides raising a family of eight, being the town telephone operator, and working the switchboard from her dining room, Nellie's true fame was her beautiful flower garden.

Though her garden had long since been mowed over, I was determined to bring Nellie's garden back to life, and that I did, planting every flower, tree, and bush the zone could handle. It was a labor of love and total transformation. Years later, when I sold the farm, I proudly showed my buyers the purple wisteria blooms cascading the old washhouse roof line. They never imagined wisteria was possible in North Dakota, nor had I.

Over the years, I've become a woman of many passions and favorites, from flowers, birds, critters, books, and even antique garden tools. One prized possession is an old hand hammered scoop I use for filling the bird feeders. It has perfect balance; it is so beautiful that if I close my eyes, I can imagine the old Smithy pounding out its smooth exactness, making it a thing of beauty. Years ago, I bought an old trowel at an antique shop; it fits perfectly in my hand and is worn in just the right places by the previous gardener. I once lent it to a neighbor, and when she returned it, she said, "You may think this sounds silly, but I felt an odd energy when I held the trowel in my hand." I understood the sensation completely, as only a fellow gardener could.

Spiritually, I owe much to the many years of dirt on my hands, mainly the understanding that I didn't create gardens; they created me. It only takes one seed to begin the journey, and flowers will teach us everything we need to know. The greatest gift I can give myself is time spent in the garden. I've learned patience; no matter how often we stumble, rebirth comes each spring. Most importantly, like the world, a garden's true beauty comes with a diversity of plants and colors, and I frequently say without apology, "I'm sorry I can't make it today. I'm working in my garden."

Flore II: Emily's Garden
In the Midwest, our gardens sleep in winter, but I've never believed the world of gardens and flowers is limited by the days or weeks they bloom. Instead, I find the charms of a garden can come during the coldest days of winter.

After months of frozen ground covered in white, I know it's time to transport myself to the garden of daydreams. I make a cup of tea, move to the bookshelf near the fireplace, and choose one of the many well-worn and much-loved gardening books. Opening these literary riches allowed me to walk and tour gardener's journal pages. Today, my choice was Emily Dickinson, and after an hour of reading, I was spellbound by her descriptions of aromatic vintage roses and perfumed artemisia. Her fragrant world ignites my imagination, and I dreamily walk alongside Emily in her garden. We were calm and unruffled as our summer gowns brushed the pebbled path, and her excited dog, Carlo, dashed ahead of us chasing birds. Lazily, we linger to examine and smell each new bloom. The sun is warm as our shawls drop from our shoulders, and we laugh, sharing gardening secrets. Emily claims eggshells will keep slugs away and promises to read her latest poem to me at teatime, but alas, the sound of my doorbell brings me back to earth and the blistery realities of winter. When the last of the snow melts and spring arrives, I wake at dawn anxious to get my hands in the soil. The thawed earth makes me far too busy for the garden books that had stirred my imagination in January. A spade now fills my hand until winter comes again.

FLORE III: MY FAVORITE GARDENER

My favorite gardener was my Aunt Norma Jean, who once said she'd never met a gardener she didn't like. Her many letters always expressed one wish: to be in my garden helping me weed. I told her that weeding was my least favorite part of being a gardener, and in her following letter, she explained the merits and rewards of weeding. *Weeding lets you see your plants at ground level, their plight, and the insects they invite; you get to know them at ground level, which is much more rewarding than looking down at them.* From then on, weeding became a joy, as was the flutter of a bumble bee's wings near my cheek, a butterfly perched on my hat, and eye-to-eye contact with the numerous dragonflies and tiny green frogs sunning peacefully on black-eyed Susans. I've always been thankful for her words that turned the weeding chore into a delightful practice.

After my aunt died at 103, she continued to touch my gardening life. When I left my beloved farm in February, taking any of my cherished plants with me was impossible, but I was sure I'd be able to replace them. By summer, my new garden was an explosion of iris, lilies, roses, seeds from friends in England, assorted lavender plants, anemones, English daisies, and watercress. Still, one of my favorite perennials was missing: the yellow Clematis macropetala that had draped a patio trellis at the farm. I looked everywhere to no avail; the ironic thing about the now elusive Clematis macropetala seed was I used to collect them every fall and mail them to friends and relatives, bragging about their beauty and dandelion-puffball seed heads. Unfortunately, I had failed to save the seeds for myself. Months after my Aunt Norma Jean passed, her family sent me a package containing all my letters to her. One night, feeling somewhat melancholy, I retrieved the letters and began to read them. As I opened one letter, a little packet fell onto my lap. It was in my handwriting and said, Clematis Macropetala seeds.

Flore IV: Separated from the Earth

I feared depression coming on; for many days, feeling empty, as though I were sleepwalking through life. Unconscious and zombie-like as I wheeled the trash bins to the curb or stood in line for groceries, I even caught myself at our local thrift shop reaching to buy an item of clothing I had recently donated. I wanted to scream, but even that required an energy beyond me.

Today, I woke up at seven, made coffee, and went outside to water the thirsty lawn; the lack of rain also disheartened me; the weeks of drought and intense heat hadn't helped my frame of mind. Soon, the water pushed through the hose and into the sprinkler, and as it spouted high into the air, it caught the sun's rays, looking like thousands of sparkling diamonds. I wasn't the only one to notice; no sooner had the artificial rain shower begun its dance, suddenly various birds appeared for a morning shower, and I felt grateful that I could relieve them from the morning's heat. A part of me was tempted to shed my clothes and join them.

With my little dog, Peaches, I headed to the garden in the backyard. As we turned the corner, I was stunned to see the garden arbor crowned with beautiful lavender morning glories reaching for the sun. It was a magnificent site, which I had failed to see, having stayed indoors to escape the heat. I stood back to admire what had started as a simple design scribbled on paper into this glorious reality, reminding me if you plant it, it will grow. The many birds that had gathered and the beauty of the morning glories renewed my *joie de vivre*, and I retrieved a basket and weeder from the shed to begin long-neglected chores. I got on my knees, and as the weeds surrendered, I surrendered my melancholy, knowing the only thing wrong with me was that I'd separated myself from the earth for too long.

Gardens will beckon like ravenous lovers, needing constant attention, but to love a garden is to know life's greatest secrets. Gardening has taught me to weed out negative thoughts and nurture dreams – think of the dreams in a tiny seed just waiting to be awakened. I look at every flower, knowing it's a reminder to blossom.

William's Red Roses

Lynda McKinney Lambert

EARLY MORNING IS MY favorite time of day. My habit is to walk into the bathroom, pull up the blind, and peer outside to see what this new day is like. When I looked out the window early this morning, it was not yet daylight. The world was a soft, hazy, grayish blue. Snow! Newly fallen snow covered the earth like a pristine, frigid blanket. The wind was not blowing, and the fresh day seemed eerily still. Even the early morning shrieks of black crows were absent. I glanced out over the wooded hillside, far beyond this second-story window. Everything was quiet. Subdued. Bleak.

A winter storm moved in yesterday, just as the weather reports predicted. By noon, the rural roads in our neighborhood were already covered with the kind of large snowflakes that quietly surrounded everything. There is something about the anticipation of a snowstorm that stirs us to remember our childhood.

"Oh, this is the perfect snowstorm! It's the kind of snowfall that I love," I shouted to my husband, Bob. "It is exactly the kind of crisp, cold winter day that makes me so excited. I feel like I am a little child when I see this snow," I continued to tell him. I admit I am nostalgic when snow brings layers of distant memories back to my mind. Memories of past years arrived with the snow. They are like a child's building blocks, tumbling down one over another. Thoughts of childhood mingle with the aromas in my mother's kitchen on distant winter days as I peered through the fogged-up windowpane.

On winter days, my mother, Esther, often baked chocolate chip cookies, yeast breads, and pumpkin pies for the family. She knew her four children would be hungry when they came home from school in the late afternoon. We smelled the fragrances of her baking as we opened the back door into the kitchen.

In the early 1950s, Esther could have been one of the women in the magazine advertisements. Mom might have been Betty Crocker. She wore a freshly ironed cotton house dress as she cleaned, cooked, and sang hymns as she moved through the house. She had a clear alto voice and the people at our little Methodist church always requested that she sing something special in church some Sundays. I can close my eyes and still hear my mother's voice as she sings, "I come to the garden alone, while the dew is still on the roses."

I have no memories of my mother wearing anything but a cotton dress every day. She wrapped a starched and ironed pastel gingham apron around her waist. The apron covered the front of her dress when she was cooking. Later, when I was in high school, Mom expanded her wardrobe and occasionally wore a pair of slacks.

We grew up knowing for sure that our mother was a lady. It had nothing to do with our humble economic status. Prior to the 1960s a lady would never think of wearing anything but a dress every day to do her household chores and cooking for her family.

Yesterday, my own kitchen was warmer than usual. The room smelled like sweet, ripe, red cherries and spicy cinnamon. I opened the oven door a little at a time to let the hot, fragrant vapors escape and warm the room around me. I put on oven mitts, reached into the hot oven, and slowly, steadily, pulled out the piping hot glass baking dish. This was the perfect day to bake cherry crisps! Before it had a chance to cool, I dug a soup spoon deep into the cherry crisp and removed a little dish of the sweetness. I told myself, *"Just a little taste!"*

As I lifted the warm, red cherry delight to my mouth, I reflected on the snow outside the windows, noticing how it had accumulated on the old, weathered gray fence that surrounds the yard. The oak fence was built by my husband, Bob, our children, and some of their strong, male teenage friends in the summer of 1977. The fence surrounded the swimming pool built that spring. Every year since then, in springtime, the fence becomes the backdrop for the perennials when they begin to bloom.

Why is it that on solitary winter days, distant memories come calling?

Today, I felt transported to a particular sparkling day in August. It was my birthday; my father gave me a red rose bush in a black plastic container. Thin roots burst out from holes in the bottom of that container. I knew the rose bush desperately needed to be planted so it could thrive, but I was so young and busy taking care of my large family and did not take the time to appreciate the gift. I did not plant it for a couple more years. This particular memory makes me feel so disappointed in myself. Because of my neglect, the bush did not flourish, and it did not bloom. A rose bush is meant to be planted by just such a fence as I had, so that it could bloom and twine upwards toward the morning light.

Over fifty summers have passed since my father gave me that red rose bush. Once it was finally nestled in the rich, dark earth next to the wooden fence, I never had the heart to dig it up, even though it never bloomed. I left it there as a reminder that time passes rapidly, and one day it is too late to say, "thank you." Too late to appreciate some gifts we received when we were young. A dull sorrow always took root in my heart when I thought of that rose bush.

As I watched the snow drifting this morning, onto the wooden fence, it unearthed more memories.

Last summer, I discovered something so unexpected out there on that old fence that I had to walk closer to have a better look. Could it possibly be what I was thinking it might be? Closer inspection revealed that the old rose bush my father bought me for my birthday so long ago was in full bloom! A joyous riot of deep red color wound all over the fence. The thorny, thick vine moved through the rough, weatherworn planks, from the inside of the fence to the outside. From every angle, the fully blooming roses could be seen. The tender tips of the branches reached upwards, far beyond the tops of the fence slats. It reached upwards, swaying in the sunlight of a balmy summer day. I stood entranced by those old – fashioned, deep red roses. They were wide open, with soft crimson petals flying outward. There was an inner crown of tiny little yellow pistils that looked like a circle of delicate yellow flowers surrounding the roses' centers.

My father's roses were blooming! In my great amazement, I said it aloud. "My father's red climbing roses are blooming! Oh, thank you, Dad!"

I thought about my father's birth name, William—an ancient name going back to the Teutonic ages. It is a strong name. A perfect name for a little boy who would be orphaned in childhood. A young husband who was drafted into World War II and would leave his wife and new baby girl to spend two years in freezing trenches during winter days in Europe. A hard-working father who would labor in the steel mills for a weekly paycheck to support the family he loved. A valiant man who gave the days and years of his life for the family and never expected anything in return. We learned the lessons of living a good life in the home he built for us with his own hands.

Names are important. Dad's Germanic name is Wilhelm. It can be broken down into two parts. "Will" means to desire. "Helm" is a helmet. William, my father, desired to teach his children how to live an honorable life. In order to do that, he picked up his steel lunch bucket and safety helmet in the early morning when his children were still asleep in their beds. In the darkness of the morning, Dad left for his long walk down the railroad tracks and through the woods, and finally crossed over the creek on the wooden planks of a swinging bridge to eventually reach the entrance gate of the steel mill.

Today, I know that beneath the layer of snow, just in front of the weathered fence, there is a red rose bush waiting through the silence of the wintry weather.

Sunshine will come in the spring to warm the chilled earth. The red rose bush will begin to grow once again.

Bob has turned up the radio in the warm kitchen. He is listening to the radio. I walked into the kitchen, and we embraced. My husband has a wide smile on his face. He tells me this is his favorite song,

"Thunder Rolls." We danced together to Garth Brooks singing in our warm kitchen this morning, until the song ended.

Spring did arrive as it always does, but the winter months had been unusually harsh, and we lost many plants and trees during the icy storms. William's red roses never bloomed again.

As I begin the tedious work of cleaning winter debris from my flower gardens I pause to remember my father's red roses, his carefully tended gardens, and the years of my childhood that nurtured me to become the woman I am today who tends my own gardens.

This morning, as I stepped outside to begin work in my garden, I saw that a woman was bending over one of the purple flowers. She told me she was taking pictures to send to her mother in California. Occasionally, as I am outside working in the gardens, a car will go by and then slow down, and a driver will call out to me, "I love your gardens." I smile and say, "Thank you."

At that moment, my heart quietly whispers, "Dad, you would be so proud of me."

Growing

Carol Raitt

SPRING IN THE PACIFIC Northwest makes me feel giddy with joy. Each day brings a new shade of green. Chartreuse leaves unfurl like tiny fans on my vine maples. Trilliums poke their noses up through dark soil. People emerge from their homes to greet the sunshine. Dandelions arise from the ground and lift their saffron faces to the sky. Neighbors strike up back fence tête-à-têtes. Crow couples snap slender twigs from my trees for nest-building. It is a time to plan outings with friends—hikes and bird-watching trips. A time to consider new plants for the garden. But when spring 2020 arrived, life—inside and out—was very different from past years.

In December 2019, a mysterious new virus erupted in China. Less than a month later, the first confirmed case of Covid-19 in the U.S. appeared in Washington state. The deadly virus spread worldwide and on March 11—eight days before the spring equinox—the World Health Organization declared a Covid-19 pandemic. Life halted in Seattle and the rest of the world and as the daylight hours lengthened, my life and activities felt foreshortened. I looked outside at two raised bed garden boxes—beds unplanted for five years. Perhaps this was my year to grow vegetables. When I looked at the bare soil I felt renewed interest, a longing to watch life emerge from the fallow beds. Though I am no stranger to gardening, my approach to growing vegetables has always been scattershot. My attitude has been *if it lives, it lives; if it doesn't, oh well*. My vegetable gardens usually result in more misfires than successes. That was about to change. In a world that felt smaller and more restricted, I'd nurture my physical and mental health by channeling my energy into growing tomatoes, carrots, lettuce, beets, and kale. And this time I would do it right.

A few years after my husband and I married we bought our first home, a 1950s mid-century rambler, north of Seattle. I fell in love with the park-like massive front yard with its towering 100-year-old Douglas fir trees. Sam was enamored with a one-quarter acre, backyard parcel where the previous owners had grown vegetables. Within one month of moving into our new home Sam's first issue of *Organic Gardening* magazine arrived in the mail. When most young men might be dreaming of buying a motorcycle, my husband had his eye on a rototiller. That's when I knew he was serious. I tried to be supportive, but I could not fully buy into his passion for gardening. I was caring for our newborn, so my gardening efforts focused on weed-pulling and diverting our Airedale terrier from digging up and devouring entire rows of carrots.

Sam's dedicated garden work paid off. He grew enough vegetables to supply a food bank. From midsummer through early fall I prepped carrots, beans, and corn for our new upright freezer—an appliance purchased for our surfeit of fresh produce. I couldn't bear to see food go to waste. My grandmother canned everything she grew, but I was not my grandmother. I was paranoid I'd poison our family, so our freezer became my go-to for food preservation.

As a child I spent most summer days with my grandparents. Their home provided love, stability, and escape from my parent's alcohol-fueled battles. As a child I didn't know my grandmother's respect for nature and her love of gardening would work its way into my young soul and foster my own love of nature.

Grandma and I worked outside in her garden each day during the growing season. When grandma picked pole beans, she put a faded cloth babushka over her short-cropped white hair. "To keep the bugs off," she told me. Grandma's hands fascinated me. So large and strong. So cool against my face. So gentle. These were the hands that picked beans, dug potatoes, staked raspberry vines, made soap, scrubbed clothes, kneaded bread, canned peaches, knit sweaters, and patched my jeans. The top of her hand was as pale and translucent as onion skin. Her fingertips and palms revealed a network of deeply etched lines and wrinkles. And yet her hands were smooth, as if every bit of roughness had been erased by the love she put into her many years of hard work and the decades she'd spent digging in her garden.

I remember the two of us kneeling, side by side, pulling slender carrots and purple potatoes from the cool, damp soil. I learned how to wiggle and loosen the carrots so the roots would not break from the leaves. In mid-July we picked fat raspberries that grandma boiled into jam in a tall stockpot. As the berries bubbled and burst, her home filled with a sweet and heady fragrance. After she'd filled the jars and sealed them with paraffin wax I wiped away the sticky jam dribbles from the glass.

Memories rekindle as I unload bags of compost blended with chicken manure from my SUV and stack them near my raised bed gardens. My purchase of amendments from Swanson's Nursery is streamlined compared to how my grandparents procured their soil enrichments. I remember being eight years old, riding in the backseat of grandpa's 1948 Ford sedan, the three of us enroute to a poultry farm beyond Seattle's city limits. While I waited in the car my grandparents scooped raw chicken manure into buckets and loaded them into the trunk. Manure days seemed to always coincide with the first warm day of spring and in the time it took to drive home grandpa's car and its occupants stunk of manure, too.

Each bag of compost mix weighs forty pounds. After I remove the sixth bag from my car I'm sweating, swearing, and short of breath. I am out of shape. My gym closed weeks ago because of the pandemic. Tonight my arms and shoulders will burn with pain, but my heart will feel good. Gardening is an act of creating. An act of love. An affirmation that life prevails, even during times of danger and uncertainty. I strive to stay upbeat. For weeks now, each day has rolled into the next with maddening monotony. Bad news. Death tolls. Negativity. I've struggled to block anxiety from creeping in but fear, like a parasite, tries to embed itself deeply, tries to sabotage my attempts to stay cheerful. As I watch the birds and other critters go about their daily business I envy their freedom and ignorance of pandemic news.

My grandmother emigrated from the former Yugoslavia to Ellis Island when she was twelve years old. I can only imagine her fear and uncertainty as she left home to travel across a vast ocean to reunite with her parents in a strange new land. She brought few possessions, but she carried a small packet of dried beans from the old country—beans sewn into the seam of her dress. The progeny of those hitchhikers were the beans grandma and I picked in her garden. Enormous, seven-inch-long, flat green beans that she cut into two-inch lengths for canning. She called them Mama's Beans. Beans she gave my husband for his first garden. Beans that I retrieved from grandma's kitchen drawer before she sold her home. Beans I safeguarded for a dozen years during Sam's many job transfers. Beans I discarded when I believed they would never be used again. Beans I now wish I had to plant in my own garden.

If grandma were alive today I would ask her questions about Mama's Beans. I wonder if she brought them to this country as a reminder of her home in Yugoslavia. Were Mama's Beans insurance for food security? Or did grandma simply enjoy eating those beans?

Once the bags of soil amendments are stacked near my garden beds I look at packets of carrot and beet seeds on my kitchen counter. I wonder if the seeds will materialize into what the package illustrations so vividly portray. The alchemy of seed becoming vegetable has always seemed mysterious and magical to me. Planting a garden requires a leap of faith and for that reason I have purchased young lettuce, kale, and tomato plants: three reliable producers in the Pacific Northwest. If nothing else I will have the makings for salad.

I am reminded of a passage from Henry David Thoreau's book, *Faith in a Seed*, which reads:

"Though I do not believe that a plant will spring up where no seed has been, I have great faith in a seed. Convince me that you have a seed there, and I am prepared to expect wonders."

How can anyone not be filled with optimism when seedlings emerge from soil? Although plant and soil scientists may not call seed germination a miracle, I am in awe of tiny carrot seeds that produce slender, orange, sweet-tasting, edible roots.

A day passes. It is a humid spring morning. I open and dump eighty pounds of amendment into the raised-bed gardens. My arms lift the spading fork. Bend, scoop, blend. Over and over I turn the soil, mixing compost into less fertile soil. A fat earthworm emerges. A good omen. As the soil darkens the smell of promise hangs in the muggy air.

Two crows in an adjacent yard saunter toward me. They eye me suspiciously. I suspect they wonder if I have displaced their overwintered food cache. Anna's hummingbirds zoom from tree branch to feeder and back. I hear the trill of a Bewick's wren. Seeing and hearing the neighborhood birds gladdens my heart. I have always found birds to be excellent companions and a chorus of songbirds confirms I am not alone in the world.

As I lift the soil I think about the millions of microorganisms in the planting bed. Unseen helpers who provide nourishment and a healthy foundation for plants to thrive. Also unseen, yet very much present in my heart and mind, is the spirit of my grandmother. I feel her guidance and inspiration as I create this garden. In a world that feels uncertain and scary this one patch of soil holds potential. A chance to create something from nothing and nurture new life.

I open the packet of carrot seeds and sprinkle them into a shallow trough, then cover the seeds with a dusting of soil. I say a prayer that the finches and sparrows won't eat the seeds. I dream of slender, sturdy, perfect carrots developing below their headdresses of feathery green leaves; worms aerating the soil while meandering through an underground obstacle course of root vegetables. No carrot-foraging Airedale will disturb this garden. Next to the carrots I sow half a packet of beet seeds. How can a root so robust and round materialize from such a tiny seed? I transfer one sturdy tomato plant from the nursery pot into loam, then set in twelve small plantlets of lettuce and kale and water them gently. It is April 22, 2020.

After two weeks, the beet seeds germinate, the kale stands strong, and the romaine is forming new leaves—where are the carrots? I am about to replant the row but three days later I see a mass of green. Carrot seedlings. I did not inherit my grandma's patience and her faith in things unseen. Grandma would smile. "Just wait." I feel her assurance that with love and care I will reap a bountiful harvest.

Spring slips into summer. The garden thrives. Yes, I grumble about thinning the carrots—a recurring obligation that becomes interesting only when the smallest, tenderest carrots are worth nibbling. I tire of searching for baby slugs nestled within lettuce leaves before I prepare a salad. It is all part of gardening. Hard green orbs droop from tomato vines corralled by a circular, wire hoop designed to keep the plant from toppling under the weight of its fruit. I pinch a tomato leaf and smell my fingers. Tomatoes are in the nightshade family. Their leaves are poisonous to eat but their fragrance is intoxicating. I will wait weeks before the fruits ripen but today I dream of sun-warmed, salted tomatoes and sharp cheddar sandwiched between slices of rustic sourdough and I imagine my blender whirring the juicy red fruits, chopped cucumbers, peppers, onions, cilantro, salt, pepper, and olive oil into my favorite summer elixir: chilled gazpacho.

The kale grows taller, its sturdy leaves irresistible to cabbage white butterflies. To some gardeners they're pests (their velvety green larvae devour the leaves of plants in the cabbage family), but I enjoy watching them flutter from one plant to another and I don't mind sharing my bounty. Another lesson my grandmother taught me as a child: hurt no living thing. I try my best, but arachnids and slugs challenge my relationship with the creepy-crawly world.

The beets and carrots are ready to harvest in July. The first ripe tomatoes appear in early August. I am amazed how the garden flourished, how a very ordinary undertaking became special and reawakened meaningful memories of my childhood and my grandma. Memories that comforted me during a time when pandemic-induced fear and danger felt like two evil twins hell-bent on subverting joy and erasing possibilities.

Summer is barely over before I begin thinking about next year's garden. Perhaps I'll put in scarlet-runner-beans, reliable climbers whose vermillion flowers attract hummingbirds—a double bonus: birds and beans. Or lemon cucumber. Thai eggplant? I once laughed when Sam pored over pages of *Organic Gardening* magazine. Now I read articles about companion planting while I await next season's Territorial Seed catalogue. Though some people in the Northwest grow winter vegetables, my garden and I will take a break until next spring.

Mid-September. It is a few days until the autumn equinox. I must remove the fading tomato vines, weed near the remaining Tuscan kale, and protect six new lettuce starts from slugs and snails. The days are cooler and damp. Each day's sunset dims the sky earlier than it did the day before. I miss my morning watering routine. I miss the earthy smell of carrots pulled from warm soil and observing how the textures and colors of kale next to lettuce leaves next to beet greens change with the movement of the sun.

Already I find myself nostalgic for the season that has passed. I feel grateful to have rekindled a connection to my garden. Thankful for the deep satisfaction that comes from tilling soil, growing food, and observing the wild birds who pass through my yard. I know, of course, I cannot take full credit for this year's garden successes. I thank my grandma for her wisdom: in gardening and in life. These are exquisite gifts in troubling times.

The Charms of Botanical Gardens

Elizabeth Kenneday

JOURNAL ENTRY: Monday afternoon, April 23, 2018—Pisac, Peru: *The cactus gardens were extraordinary. Made me so happy—what is it about botanical gardens?*

I WROTE THAT WHILE travelling in Peru with a group of twenty women writers hiking the famed Inca ruins while visiting the renowned Quechua women weavers of the high Andes. Rather than shopping one afternoon, two of us opted for the rare treats that awaited us at the Felipe Marin Moreno Botanic Garden. Created in 1917 by Moreno, the garden focuses on Peruvian native plants, including 200 of Peru's 3,000 potato plant varieties. This visit was one of the highlights of the trip for me.

I adore botanical gardens. I seek them out wherever I go. I've often wondered why I'm so captivated by them. They exist in many forms from the sixteen exquisite, themed Huntington Botanical Gardens spread over 130 acres in San Marino, California, to the delightfully quirky Gladys Merrick Garden situated in the dusty desert town of Ridgecrest, California, at the Maturango Museum. These gardens, defined in contemporary times by Botanic Gardens Conservation International as "institutions holding documented collections of living plants for the purpose of scientific research, conservation, display and education," is an accurate but skeletal and dry description that leaves out the varied pleasures found in these gardens.

There is some debate about the earliest physic gardens that cultivated herbs and medicinal plants, preceding modern botanical gardens. It is said that Aristotle had a physic garden at the Lyceum in Athens, Greece, in the fourth century BC for educational purposes, and Pliny the Elder, in the first century CE, mentions the garden of botanist and pharmacologist Antonius Castor in Rome, Italy. Physic gardens flourished in medieval times, containing mostly vegetables, but also medicinal plants. These plants were sectioned into geometric patterns and labelled. This tradition carries into our present-day gardens, and is one of the things I appreciate—being able to identify what I'm looking at appeals to the academic in me. The ordering and arrangement of the specimens in these gardens began to take on lovely designs, another attribute that the artist in me finds uplifting.

As global exploration began expanding in the fifteenth century, plants were being collected for scientific experimentation and learning, with more gardens becoming attached to universities, medical schools, and libraries. Specimens world-wide were being collected not only for their scientific importance, but for their exoticism and beauty as well. The Renaissance era in Europe began to construct exquisite gardens, creating a cultural phenomenon that drew the public to them.

This sort of twinning of science, learning, and beauty with the delight of living plants creates an ambience that is hard for me to resist. Botanical gardens have maintained the historical components of labelling, experimentation, and learning aspects, but added an enriching social quality and expansion in scope. These characteristics can be seen at the famed Huntington Library, Art Museum, and Botanical Gardens complex. Begun in 1903 when Henry E. Huntington purchased the San Marino Ranch, the gardens presently contain over 83,000 living plants, including rare and endangered species. A botanical conservation and research facility are housed on the grounds. The gardens are so numerous and spread over such a vast area that I've only been able to visit three so far—and they were stunning!

Rivalling the Huntington Botanical Gardens in scope are the twenty-four acre Denver Botanic Gardens. I was travelling in Greece with a few friends who all live in Denver. As I had a lengthy layover there before my flight home, one of them, who shares my love of botanical gardens, suggested we go for a visit and lunch at the stunning gardens in her city while waiting for my departure. I was enthralled by the extent of the gardens, the architectural elements, the art gallery and library—even a School of Botanical Art & Illustration which immediately caught my interest, though not feasible for me to engage at that time. The standout in the short time I was able to spend at the gardens was the exquisite lily pond.

The smaller, yet unique garden at the Maturango Museum contains mature xeriscaping with both native and non-native plants that minimize water use, and an informative demonstration garden. Desert tortoise habitat and a recycling water fountain for birds have been fabricated for the benefit of the local wildlife. Whimsical metal sculptures refer to the sheepherding history and the nearby Coso Petroglyphs, and cultural artifacts from the area's mining, ranching, and farming past are found throughout the grounds. A human sundial invites delightful time telling using one's own shadow.

My favorite feature is the labyrinth constructed of locally sourced tufa and said to be "modeled after the classic seven-circuit design first seen in Crete more than 3500 years ago." Walking the labyrinth calmed my nervousness before giving a book talk in the museum's auditorium before a surprisingly large audience. A sun hat or parasol is highly recommended when visiting!

Musical events are held in many botanical gardens; they take on an aliveness that is utterly magical. I thoroughly enjoyed a concert in the Boboli Gardens at the Medici's Pitti Palace in Florence, Italy, when studying there one summer. A Paganini concert consisting of simply a violin and a guitar was enchanting with the surrounding Renaissance statues amongst the emerald greenery and colorful flowers of the garden.

Begun in 1549 the gardens were designed originally by Niccolò Pericoli for the Duchess of Toledo, featuring geometric patterns of flowers with hedge borders and trees, rare and wild plants, and fountains. The gardens saw a succession of fantastic features added to the original design for over a century—grottos, statues, an amphitheatre, an Egyptian obelisk from Luxor and other collectables from antiquity, and so much more. Our concert was held in a more modest corner of the garden near a lovely grotto that suited the music perfectly.

Weddings have become common events at botanical gardens. I've wondered if that's because it saves on the hefty florist bill commonly associated with these festivities! I attended the wedding of one of my student lab aides at the Earl Burns Miller Japanese Garden situated on the campus of California State University, Long Beach. I could see why it's become an immensely popular venue for weddings with its bridge over the koi pond representing the joining of the happy couple. It was a lovely setting for the occasion.

I devoted much time to that garden when I was a Professor of Art there. With a worthwhile nod to multiculturism, the garden was an ideal setting for students to learn about the Japanese approach to garden aesthetics as well as provide watercolor, drawing and photographic experiences from the garden's features—a koi pond, a tea house, and its skillfully cultivated live plants. Reading the haiku poems in the traditional Japanese style created on its reflective grounds were a favorite pastime.

I spent so much time at that garden that I was invited to join the Faculty Advisory Committee. It was my favorite committee of all my years in academe. Once a month we met for tea at the tea house on the grounds to discuss possibilities for the garden in its educational function. I could've met for that committee every week as it was so restorative!

As a graduate student, I found the California Botanic Garden (then the Rancho Santiago Botanic Garden), a quiet respite from the rigors of both my MFA and PhD studies at the Claremont Graduate University. Home to Claremont Graduate University's Master's and PhD programs in Botany, the garden conserves and displays about 2,000 native California plant species. I often photographed in the garden making studies for artworks. Walking the trails through them was a contemplative experience.

At the foot of the Wrigley Memorial overlooking the sea on Catalina Island is another enchanting botanical garden. The memorial is dedicated to the memory of William Wrigley, Jr., whose vision of a protected island for future generations has allowed visitors for decades to enjoy the natural beauty of the island. The botanical garden began with Wrigley's wife Ada's extraordinary private desert plant collection in 1935. As care of the thirty-eight-acre garden shifted to the Catalina Island Conservancy in the 1970s, the public was granted more access and the plant collection shifted emphasis to those specimens endemic to the island. My husband and I walked hand in hand through the garden's pathways on our honeymoon—a treasured memory.

In a nod to the experimental gardens of antiquity and the physic gardens of medieval times, an astonishing organic garden lies improbably in the tropical jungle of Belize in Central America. Filmmaker Francis Ford Coppola began organic gardening at his Blancaneaux Lodge resort in the Cayo District in the 1990's. Frustrated by the lack of fruits and vegetables needed for the resort's restaurants, Coppola, who had already been a winemaker in California since 1978, took on the challenge of overcoming the abundant snails, white flies, and other destructive pests without using poison or pesticides to create the surprising three and one-half acre Hideaways Organic Garden. The Garden Spot Restaurant located on the grounds serves up exceptional vegetarian meals using fresh produce grown on the grounds.

We visited there when travel was just reviving after the pandemic that kept many would-be visitors at home. We were the only diners for the evening, beginning the evening's fare with cocktails and appetizers. We were treated to the fascinating story of the garden while we sipped our drinks made with fresh herbs and ate scrumptious appetizers. We were then taken on a tour of the vast rows of edibles with the head gardener, who explained the complex methods of ensuring the success of the plantings and the unique composting system in place.

As we walked among the abundant array of fruit and vegetable plants, the sun began setting. We returned to the Garden Spot Restaurant to dine under a magical full moon. A three-course meal beginning with a delightful soup and ending with a lovely dessert—all of it created from the garden's offerings, of course—was a captivating culinary experience!

The Garden at Blancaneaux Lodge proved so successful that Coppola repeated the endeavor with a smaller version at his seaside resort, The Turtle Inn, in Placencia, Belize. Tours through the garden are offered, and a charming pizzeria sits at the edge of it. Fresh basil from the garden on a margarita pizza there is not to be missed!

Located in the Arboretum at the Stanford University campus, The Arizona Garden served a sanctuary role as I awaited open-heart surgery (which was quite successful) at the Stanford Medical Facility in Palo Alto. The garden was founded in 1888 by landscape architect Rudolph Ulrich who collected many of the plants from the Sonoran Desert. Leland Stanford, a garden enthusiast and then president of the Central Pacific Railroad, allowed Ulrich unlimited access to boxcars and labor while travelling through the desert where he dug up numerous specimens largely unknown to the general public at that time, from barrel cacti to yuccas. He created a surreal and well-liked garden with his collections, although his methods of acquisition would be frowned upon today.

The Arizona Garden remains an extraordinarily popular spot. As I watched from a garden bench, continuous clusters of visitors roamed the garden paths, most armed with some means of visual recording from high-end cameras to smartphones. Documenting christenings, creating engagement and family reunion portraits and the like, they waited patiently (or impatiently) for the backdrop of their choice provided by the garden's stunning specimens.

In our own hometown of Reno, Nevada, is the thirteen-acre Wilbur D. May Arboretum and Botanical Garden. May, son of the founder of the May Company Department Stores, has been described as a rancher, world traveler, aviator, artist, and philanthropist. Owner of the 2600-acre Double Diamond Ranch in South Reno from 1936 until his death in 1982, May believed in education through his arboretum and botanical gardens, using twelve themed gardens and groves to demonstrate gardening in the high desert environment together with positive conservation practices. The gardens contain more than 4,000 plant species and include artifacts from May's cattle ranch and the Basque sheepherding era. The adjacent museum exhibits fascinating objects from more than forty of his worldwide journeys. Musical and other cultural events are offered regularly, and the grounds are another popular location for weddings.

In an era when plant species are disappearing with alarming rapidity, botanical gardens provide a myriad of functions from their earliest incarnations as scientific experimental works that now serve critical conservation purposes to their cultural and educational roles in providing meaningful experiences in enchantingly curated spaces, alive with bewitching flora of every sort. The charms of botanical gardens are endlessly delightful.

About the Contributors

CAROLYN DOEPKE BENNETT is a lecturer and gardener. She has a Master's degree in the Conservation and Preservation of Historic Landscapes, Parks, and Gardens from the Architectural Association School of Architecture, London. Originally from Evanston, Illinois, she now lives in Ojai, California.

HENRI BENSUSSEN (she/her) earned a B.A. in Biology at UC Santa Cruz. Her poetry chapbook, *Earning Colors*, was published by Finishing Line Press (2015). Her essays have appeared in the anthology *Golden State 2017: The Best New Writing from California*, edited by Lisa Locascio, and the publications *Pacific Horticulture, Bridges,* and *Sinister Wisdom*, amongst others. She's a past board member of the Mendocino Coast Botanical Gardens and was a master gardener there. According to Henri, one could say we are married to our gardens. In her case, it was a romance with a trashed half-acre, devoting herself to its resurrection as a landscape offering solace and nourishment for the soul.

EM BROUSSEAU is a writer and farmer from a small seaside town. A graduate of Emmanuel College's Writing, Editing, and Publishing program, her work can be found in *The Santa Fe Literary Review* and the McFarland anthology *When Home is Not Safe: Writings on Domestic Verbal, Emotional and Physical Abuse*, among others. She currently lives in Massachusetts with her partner Beth and their bunny.

SUELLEN COX is a retired academic librarian who is passionate about reading and research, gardening, and making art. Her art practice has its foundation in lessons learned as a gardener. She creates one-of-a-kind artist's books, biblio-objects, and assemblage at her home studio in Orinda, California. Much of her artwork reflects on and celebrates the lives and contributions of women. She utilizes a variety of materials including repurposed boxes, found objects, handmade and decorative paper, ephemera, threads, paint, and ink. Text—poetics, literary fragments, and quotations—are important elements. Her work has been shown at numerous Northern California juried exhibitions.

MICHAELA EMCH is a communications and marketing specialist, translator, cultural mediator, biomimicry practitioner, creator of bio-infused solutions, safari guide, and passionate naturalist who seeks to make connections where people have not yet made them. And to do all this, she spends time outside and looks for inspiration from nature's genius.

ELIZABETH BRULÉ FARRELL's work has appeared in *The Paterson Literary Review, Poetry East, The Comstock Review, Evening Street Review, Pilgrimage, Stronger Than Fear, Unruly Catholic Feminists, Spillway, Steam Ticket, The Awakenings Review, Earth's Daughters, The Healing Muse, Except for Love: New England Poets Inspired by Donald Hall, Wild Crone Wisdom*, and *Into the Wild Garden* (for information, visit www.allynpaperworks.com) among others. She has been a recipient of the Louise Bogan Memorial Award for Poetry. She used to write advertising copy in Chicago before returning to a small coastal town in Massachusetts where she was born and her extended family resides.

DEBORAH FLEMING's nonfiction collection *Resurrection of the Wild: Meditations on Ohio's Natural Landscape* won the PEN America Diamonstein-Spielvogel Art of the Essay Award for 2020. She has published three collections of poems, most recently *Earthrise*; two chapbooks; a novel; and four volumes of scholarship. Winner of a Vandewater Poetry Award and grants from the National Endowment for the Humanities, she served for many years as director and editor of the Ashland Poetry Press.

Renée Folzenlogen comes from a long line of people who love gardens, and was raised in an interracial, interfaith, bipartisan household by kind-hearted parents with green thumbs. Her grandparents' hometown is Suzhou, China, known for exquisite gardens dating back to the 6th century, BCE. Renée is an art therapist and licensed counselor who believes in the healing power of nature. She has a tiny garden that magically expands for new plants every season, and has publishing credits in the *NY Times*, and *The Sun* magazine. Renée's father kept pet crickets as a young boy and would have enjoyed the adventures of Babycakes.

Stephani Hemness sprouted in the Evergreen State, where she still grows today. She is a recent Master of Arts graduate of Professional and Creative Writing from Central Washington University. Her writing can be found in *Manastash, Stratus, ThurstonTalk,* and on her WordPress blog. She enjoys hiking the mountains, walking the beach, and live theater.

Elizabeth Kenneday, an Emeritá Professor of Art at California State University in Long Beach, holds an MFA in Painting and Photography and a PhD in Critical Theory in Art from the Claremont Graduate University. A Fulbright Scholar recipient at the University of Iceland, her activities in environmental education through art led to numerous lectures at international conferences. Her award-winning artworks, including a Julia Margaret Cameron award, have been exhibited internationally and widely collected. She has contributed short stories and chapters to several anthologies, and her book, *Regarding Mono Lake: Novelty and Delight at an Inland Sea*, received an Eric Hoffer Finalist Award.

Lynda McKinney Lambert writes and creates visual art from her vintage home in the village of Wurtemburg, in Western Pennsylvania. She writes poetry and personal nonfiction essays. She currently has six published books, available at all retail booksellers. Her artworks have appeared in international exhibitions, including Japan, New Guinea, and the United States. Lynda retired from her position as Professor of Fine Art and Humanities at Geneva College in 2008 due to profound sight loss. She invites readers to discover the subtle nuances and beauty of a physical and spiritual world as she weaves strands from history, nature, and her personal life experiences.

Connie Levesque has a BS in Wildlife Biology and an MFA in Creative Writing. Her work has appeared in *Wild Crone Wisdom*, *Wild in the City*, and other collections. She writes and gardens in Portland, Oregon.

Roxanne Lien became an international flight attendant in 1972. Retired, she moved to North Dakota and wrote for several county newspapers. Roxanne now resides in Roseville, Minnesota, and sometimes writes under Penelope Page. She is working on her first novel, *Sleuths with Sticks*, and hopes to finish it in 2025. Her published stories and poems appear in the following: *The Willow River Anthology*, *The Nemadji Review*, Vol. 12 and Vol. 13 (University of Wisconsin-Superior literary magazine), *Soulmate Syndrome*, Vol. 1 (Wicked Shadow Press), *Wild Crone Wisdom* (aka: Penelope Page), and *Talking Stick* #32 and #33 (Jackpine Writers Bloc).

Cecile Mazzucco-Than has published in *Under the Sun*, *upstreet*, *Silk Road Review*, *VIA*, and *Connecticut Review*. She has written about her gardens since "Just the Three of Us," a childhood essay about herself, her dog, and a red-winged blackbird nesting in a willow by the pond, appeared in *Stone Soup*. Recently, "Three Trees in the City" about the towering oaks in her front yard appeared in *Stories from Where We Live: North Atlantic Coast*. When she moves, she transplants iris rhizomes from her childhood home and discovers new favorites like the Long Island Pink Camellia planted by the previous owner of her condo.

SASSAFRAS PATTERDALE is a celebrated author and Certified Professional Dog Trainer. Sassafras' books have been honored by the American Library Association, the Lambda Literary Foundation, and the Dog Writers Association of America.

CAROL RAITT is a Seattle writer, naturalist, and retired environmental educator. She has written about the Maasai in Kenya, cockroaches in Costa Rica, and sea stars off the Oregon coast. Her essays have been anthologized in *The North Coast Squid, Green Prints,* and *The Outrider Press*. Recent work appears in *Shark Reef, The Corvus Review,* and *Plate of Pandemic*. She has essays forthcoming in the journals *Canary* and *under the gum tree*. As of this writing, her garden's carrots, scallions, and romaine lettuce are healthy and growing.

A poet and librarian, **JIE TIAN** practices EarthArts through gardening, writing, and ink/paper/book making and by tending a small garden on the ancestral land of the Tongva-Gabrielino people. Her poetry and prose have appeared in literary journals and books. She served as co-editor of the Community of Writers' 2010 poetry anthology and *Open Doors: An Invitation to Poetry* (2016). Jie's artist books, *Native Songs* (2018), *Migration Songs* (2020), and *Are You True to Blue* (2023, materials gifted by artist Linney Wix) were part of San Diego Book Arts member exhibit. She is currently working on an artist book exploring "indigeneity."

OLUMAYOWA ANJOLAOLUWA WILLOUGHBY is a PhD Candidate in Africana Studies at Cornell University. They received their BA in Comparative Literature from Dartmouth College in 2014. Their dissertation *Hominids, Humanoids, and Humans: A Semiotic Analysis of Blackness in Turkey* explores the texts, signs, and codes that converge to confer meaning upon blackness.

ALINA ZOLLFRANK from (former) East Germany gardens and writes in the Pacific Northwest to get out of her whirring mind. Her essays and poetry have appeared or are forthcoming in *Last Leaves, Thimble, The Braided Way, Wordgathering, Feral, Two Thirds North, Red Ogre Review, Nude Bruce Review, October Hill Magazine, Psaltery & Lyre, Pulse, Halfway Down the Stairs, Reckon Review, Invisible City,* and others. She welcomes connections with other writers at zollizen.medium.com.

About the Editors

JULIE ARTMAN, MFA, MLIS, is a librarian at Chapman University and a book reviewer for Association of College and Research Libraries *Choice*. Her most recent and co-authored book *Your Craft as a Teaching Librarian: Using Acting Skills to Create a Dynamic Presence* was published in 2022. Julie is also a mindfulness facilitator and teacher, certified by UCLA's Mindful Awareness Research Center and the International Mindfulness Teachers Association.

STACY RUSSO, PhD, MA, MLIS, is committed to creating books and art for a more peaceful world. She is currently a professor of English at Santa Ana College after a long career as an academic librarian. Stacy is the author of several nonfiction books, the editor of two essay collections, a published poet, and the author/illustrator of two children's picture books. Her books have been featured on National Public Radio, Pacifica Radio, the Canadian Broadcasting System, Sirius XM Radio, KCET *Artbound*, *LA Weekly*, and various other media channels. She served as a longtime book reviewer for *Library Journal* and has over seventy published reviews, primarily in the areas of women's literature, American literature, and literary biography. Her writing has appeared in *Feminist Collections*, *Feminist Teacher*, *Serials Review*, and *American Libraries*. After years of working as a writer within the traditional publishing model, she created Wild Librarian Press in 2021 to independently publish her writing and the work of other writers.

www.ingramcontent.com/pod-product-compliance
Lightning Source LLC
Chambersburg PA
CBHW020538080526
44583CB00013B/903